The Rustle of Paul

The Rustle of Paul

Autobiographical Narratives in Romans, Corinthians, and Philippians

Scott S. Elliott

LONDON · NEW YORK · OXFORD · NEW DELHI · SYDNEY

T&T CLARK
Bloomsbury Publishing Plc
50 Bedford Square, London, WC1B 3DP, UK
1385 Broadway, New York, NY 10018, USA
29 Earlsfort Terrace, Dublin 2, Ireland

BLOOMSBURY, T&T CLARK and the T&T Clark logo are trademarks of Bloomsbury
Publishing Plc

First published in Great Britain 2020
This paperback edition published in 2021

A catalogue record for this book is available from the British Library.

A catalog record for this book is available from the Library of Congress.

ISBN: HB: 978-0-5676-7635-1
PB: 978-0-5677-0315-6
ePDF: 978-0-5676-7636-8
eBook: 978-0-5676-7638-2

Typeset by Deanta Global Publishing Services, Chennai, India

To find out more about our authors and books visit www.bloomsbury.com and
sign up for our newsletters.

for ...
without writing, whereabouts would we wander?

Contents

Acknowledgments

Regrettably, "Acknowledgments" are much like what I argue in this book concerning self-narratives: they are a discourse, a figure, a fragment. As such, they are signs of thanks and appreciation, but they inevitably fail at the very point where they succeed. Moreover, as with letters, various readers will hear in them various things. Nevertheless, they are good and necessary, meaningful and true. Therefore, I want, first of all, to thank David Clines and Sheffield Phoenix Press for inviting me, not long after publishing my first book with them, to propose another project and for accepting it so readily. I am equally thankful to Dominic Mattos and Bloomsbury/T&T Clark for later taking over the contract when Sheffield Phoenix had to briefly scale back their publication of new titles. My heartfelt appreciation goes especially to my friend Pat Bogusz, the creator of the book's cover art, which is aptly titled "Circumlavo."

I am grateful to the chairs and steering committee members of the now defunct "Biblical Criticism and Literary Criticism" section of the Society of Biblical Literature Annual Meeting for allowing me to present the paper that got this book underway and ultimately became Chapter 2. I benefited immensely from that opportunity and from the questions and comments that followed. I am also obliged to my friend and colleague at Adrian College, Melissa Stewart, who invited me to contribute a chapter to the *Festschrift* she edited in honor of George Aichele. That chapter (Scott S. Elliott, "What is Paul? Mythology and the Neutral in 1 Corinthians 9.19-23," in *Simulating Aichele: Essays in Bible, Film, Culture and Theory*, 120-39, ed. Melissa C. Stewart [Sheffield: Sheffield Phoenix Press, 2015]) became Chapter 3 of this book. It would never have been what it is without Melissa's careful reading and razor-sharp questions, or without the invaluable feedback from Tony Coumoundouros, Nathan Goetting, Linda Learman, Bethany Shepherd, Jim Spence, and Aïda Valenzuela—members of a short-lived but tremendously enjoyable and beneficial faculty writing group. I would be remiss if I did not also acknowledge and express my appreciation for the influence that George

Aichele himself has had on my interest in the writings of Roland Barthes and their relevance for thinking about biblical texts.

Most of all, I am overwhelmingly grateful and profoundly indebted to so many dear friends, family, colleagues, and students who have had a hand in this. Just as Barthes would do, I list them here in alphabetical order: Erin Casey, Jason Coker, Michal Beth Dinkler, Evelyn Elliott, Lydia Elliott, Janet Pietrowski, Lisa Richman, Jon Schwiebert, and Matt Waggoner. You know the respective roles you have played—gently (or not-so-gently) prodding me along, helping me work through ideas, listening to me think out loud about the book's content and especially about writing it and all that accompanies that ordeal, commiserating with me, for saying it better than I ever could and then letting me use your words, *for the long conversation*—and you know that neither these acknowledgments nor the book do justice either to you or to what you have given me. I will never forget, and I am looking forward to more.

Abbreviations

BibInt	Biblical Interpretation
HTR	Harvard Theological Review
JBL	Journal of Biblical Literature
JSNT	Journal for the Study of the New Testament
NTS	New Testament Studies
NovT	Novum Testamentum

The Novelistic Self

The August–September 2011 edition of *Peloton* magazine featured an article by John Madruga titled "Roland Barthes on the Tour" in which the author turns to Barthes's essay "The Tour de France as Epic"[1] to illustrate how the French, "informed by a more philosophical influence," view the race as "something far greater than an extreme physical undertaking."[2] That "something far greater" is, according to Madruga, "a complex combination of expression/intention, form/essence, man/nature, attacking/waiting, and natural/artificial [whereby] the Tour de France is a language unto itself, a chain of signification, ever evolving, ever changing, taking shape, like a novel, toward a final conclusion, sentence and period."[3] Andy Stafford describes *Mythologies* as "a form of social psychoanalysis that looked at the way in which our minds—in a bid to give ourselves some kind of meaning, purpose and even disalienation— actively participated in self-delusions."[4] Barthes sought to unravel, in these fifty-three short reflections on various randomly and arbitrarily selected "figures of rhetoric" drawn from everyday French life, the conflation and confusion of "Nature" and "History" by exposing "in the decorative display of what-goes-without-saying the ideological abuse [he] believed was hidden there."[5] He describes the Tour de France as a total and ambiguous myth that is simultaneously expression and projection, realistic and utopian.[6] Madruga, on the other hand, unwittingly reinscribes the mythology of *Le Tour*, taking the clarity and assurance proffered by so many narratives of the race, always varied

---

[1] Roland Barthes, *Mythologies: The Complete Edition, in a New Translation*, trans. Richard Howard and Annette Lavers (1957; New York: Hill and Wang, 2012), 122–33.
[2] John Madruga, "Roland Barthes on the Tour," *Peloton* 5 (August–September, 2011): 100.
[3] Madruga, "Roland Barthes on the Tour," 105.
[4] Andy Stafford, *Roland Barthes* (London: Reaktion Books, 2015), 60–61.
[5] Barthes, *Mythologies*, xi.
[6] Barthes, "Tour de France as Epic," *Mythologies*, 130.

and nuanced but fundamentally the same, as being indicative of what the race really is, or what it actually does, as if for its own sake or, in other words, by its very nature. Whereas Barthes tells the story of the story, Madruga merely repeats, recasts, and reaffirms the story.[7]

Despite the fact that so many professional bicycle races contain the word "tour" in their title, the Tour de France is the only one that is regularly referred to as, simply, "the Tour." It is not merely an abbreviation but a metonymy. And, interestingly enough, "The Tour de France as Epic" focuses on how the proper names of the racers so familiar to followers of both the sport and the event function as metonymies in their own right. Barthes describes how the Tour, as "a world of characterial essences . . . posited by a sovereign nominalism which makes the racer's name the stable depository of an eternal value . . . is an uncertain conflict of certain essences," and "nature, customs, literature, and rules successively relate these essences to each other . . . and it is from this interplay that the epic is born."[8] Similarly, the name Paul functions metonymically in the discourse of professional biblical interpreters as well as in that of many ordinary readers, both of which imbue the name, the author's identity, the authenticity of the writing subject, with a certain validity, authority, power. "Paul" is a cipher, shorthand not only for an historical figure, a character, a writer, a system of thought, a body of work, and so on. It also, and more importantly, serves as the encodement of a special blend encompassing all these things, as well as ideologies of the self, the individual, identity, authorship, and more. Paul and his letters are merged into a fraught and overwrought mythology, an overdetermined narrative that, like *Le Tour*, is a curious amalgamation of the "realistic and utopian at the same time." The perfectly ordinary, occasional, and practical nature of Paul's letters, by virtue of their collectivity and canonicity, come to embody something that apparently transcends the mundane. Meanwhile, in the name Paul, figure and fantasy are conjoined and become one, as the writer of letters is transmogrified from phenomenon to myth.[9]

[7] See Barthes, "Myth Today," in idem., *Mythologies*, 215–74; Roland Barthes "Change the Object Itself: Mythology Today," in idem., *Image/Music/Text*, trans. Stephen Heath (1971; New York: Hill & Wang, 1977), 165–69.
[8] Barthes, "Tour de France as Epic," *Mythologies*, 130.
[9] See Stafford, *Phenomenon and Myth*, 5–7. "Phenomenon or Myth?" is not included in Barthes's *Mythologies*, though there are other myths in the collection that echo and illustrate what Stafford describes (e.g., "Racine is Racine," 106–08).

Like all of Barthes's mythologies, "The Tour of France as Epic" occupies and ponders the intersection of history and narrative, implicitly considering what it is that transforms fictions into discourses, how it does so, and to what end. Barthes also considered the texts of history and modes of historical writing vis-à-vis fiction in his essay, "The Discourse of History,"[10] which, among other things, is concerned with the conundrum of how to situate writers in relation to their own time. This is a critical issue given the understandable, sometimes necessary, often justified, but never any less problematic dependence on and drive toward "historical context" that characterizes the work of biblical scholars. The "phenomenon" of which Barthes speaks is what we so often imagine ourselves to be concerned with and in pursuit of, while the "myth" is, in part, the story of its reception. There is, then, an inherent and nearly (if not altogether) inescapable paradox: any attempt to access and to speak of the phenomenon is inevitably to participate (or at least to risk participating) in the ongoing construction and perpetuation of the myth. To take notice of the historical figure is to do so because it is already lost, its existence now only maintained by the myth that supplements and supplants it. It is, therefore, fitting that Barthes would say elsewhere, "All biography is a novel which does not dare say its name."[11]

Stafford appeals to Barthes's "belief in the Brechtian idea that we should think through other people's minds and they through ours" in order to recognize the "dialogue" that "emphasises the *circulation* (rather than ownership) of ideas."[12] The end result is not comprehensive, much less exhaustive, which itself is an effort to sidestep the sweep toward myth because "there is no more powerful constructor of 'myth' than a posthumous account, if only because there is no chance for the subject to reply."[13] What we might possibly find in the fragmentary and unsystematizable "biographemes," and between the phenomenon and myth, is "an existence ultimately as a 'trace,'

[10] Roland Barthes, "The Discourse of History," in idem., *The Rustle of Language*, trans. Richard Howard (1967; Berkeley: University of California Press, 1989), 127–40.
[11] Roland Barthes, *OCii*, 1307; cited in and translated by Andy Stafford, *Roland Barthes: Phenomenon and Myth* (Edinburgh: Edinburgh University Press, 1988), 190f.
[12] Stafford, *Phenomenon and Myth*, 6.
[13] Ibid., 6–7. Cf. Jane Gallop, *The Deaths of the Author: Reading and Writing in Time* (Durham: Duke University Press, 2011); Jacques Derrida, "The Deaths of Roland Barthes," in idem., *The Work of Mourning*, eds. Pascale-Anne Brault and Michael Naas (1981; Chicago: University of Chicago Press, 2001), 31–68.

contradictory but none the less tangible."[14] Once we consider that Paul never appears to have written anything resembling a formal or intentional, much less extended, autobiography but instead scattered pieces and versions and postures of himself throughout his letters, which are incomplete and often fragmentary in their own right, Paul, his letters, and treatments of both by New Testament scholars become exemplary texts for the sort of exploration I aim to undertake in this book. The relevance and utility of Barthes's writing for thinking about "Paul's" autobiographical fragments is not so much that Paul thought of himself specifically, or the self generally, in the same manner (though, perhaps he did), but rather that it resonates with, and is better suited to, how we as readers actually encounter and experience "Paul" in Romans, Corinthians, and Philippians wherein we find "no novel (though a great deal of the fictive)."[15]

Barthes seemed to hold a "(utopian) belief in the possibility of not being socially determined, or 'classified' in social terms"[16] that I think resonates with the writer of texts like 1 Corinthians 9 and Philippians 3. Moreover, just as for Barthes, the writer of these letters sought this transience and liberty through writing: "To write the same things to you is not troublesome to me" (Phil. 3:1a).[17] To be sure, it was not literary writing on literature, as in the case of Barthes, but it was writing all the same. For the one we call Paul, writing was the very mark of the self (1 Cor. 16:21). For him, even Moses was a writer (Rom. 10:5). In the scratching and grazing that is writing, whereby marks are etched upon the palimpsestic surface of the page, the grain of the self[18] takes shape.

---

[14] Stafford, *Phenomenon and Myth*, 7.

[15] Roland Barthes, *A Lover's Discourse: Fragments*, trans. Richard Howard (New York: Hill & Wang, 1978), 7.

[16] Stafford, *Roland Barthes*, 111. Barthes himself preferred the word "atopia" to "utopia" because the former suggests "a drifting habitation" while "utopia is reactive, tactical, literary, it proceeds from meaning and governs it" (Roland Barthes, *Roland Barthes by Roland Barthes*, trans. Richard Howard [Berkeley: University of California Press, 1977], 49). It is quite possible that this resonates even more closely with some of what we find in letters attributed to Paul, as I hope to show.

[17] *Graphō* appears in one form or another some sixty-one times in the so-called authentic letters of Paul.

[18] I am alluding here to Barthes's essay, "The Grain of the Voice," in idem., *Image/Music/Text*, 179–89 (1972), wherein Barthes explores the possibility of a non-adjectival criticism and semiotics of music using, in part, Kristeva's concepts of the pheno-text and the geno-text. He describes the "grain" as "the body in the voice as it sings, the hand as it writes, the limb as it performs" (188). It is akin, therefore, to Barthes's understanding of the fragment in *Lover's Discourse*, 3–4: "The word is to be understood, not in its rhetorical sense, but rather in its gymnastic or choreographic acceptation; in short, in the Greek meaning: σχῆμα is not the 'schema,' but in a much livelier way, the body's gesture caught in action and not contemplated in repose: the body of athletes, orators, statues: what

This is an eclectic book. I mean that both as the word is understood in common usage (with my emphasis being not only a diversity of ideas, but especially a variety of sources and *tastes*) and in the more classical philosophical sense (i.e., not belonging to or representative of any school of thought but characterized by pastiche and bricolage reflective of my own inclinations). My aim is not to *apply* Barthes to Paul, or Barthes's work to Paul's letters, nor is it to make a sustained argument concerning how one *should* read self-narrative statements in the New Testament letters of Paul, much less to make any claims concerning who the "real" Paul was vis-à-vis either his ideas or the history and historical context of earliest Christianity. If anything, I aim to imitate Barthes: largely forgoing thesis, argument, proof, demonstration in favor of illustration, gloss, gesture toward, *reading and writing with*. The reason for this is that I think it is actually well suited to both the way we encounter the writer of these letters (fragmented and composite) and to certain aspects of the way this writer seemed to envision himself and others, at times. But this is not what Barthes referred to as "Neither/Nor criticism."[19] Instead, by imitating, experimenting, thinking and reading *with* and *in the light of* these diverse intertexts that come to mind and resonate,[20] I hope to follow Barthes's lead in forgoing a "science of literature" in favor of writing wherein "all language deployed by the critic [is] now part of the problem of the language used in the (literary) text under consideration."[21]

Neil Badmington writes in *The Afterlives of Roland Barthes* that his book "reads Barthes and it puts Barthes to work in the analysis of a text."[22] Similarly, this book reads the writer of the letters to the Romans, the Corinthians, and

---

in the straining body can be immobilized," and it is concerned with the materiality of language. With respect to this book, "the grain of the self" is an attempt to name what lies at the split between the "historical Paul," and so many figurations of "Paul" (e.g., characterizations, receptions, nominations, reconstructions, theologizations, and so forth).

[19] Barthes, "*Neither/Nor* Criticism," in idem., *Mythologies*, 161–64. See Chapter 3 below.

[20] Barthes, *Lover's Discourse*, 8: ". . . pieces of various origin have been 'put together. . . . And there are some which come from my own life." Cf. Roland Barthes, *The Pleasure of the Text*, trans. Richard Howard (New York: Hill & Wang, 1975), 35–36: "Reading a text cited by Stendahl . . . I find Proust in one minute detail. Elsewhere, but in the same way, in Flaubert, it is the blossoming apple trees of Normandy which I read *according to* Proust . . . this does not mean that I am in any way a Proust 'specialist': Proust is what comes to me, not what I summon up; not an 'authority,' simply a *circular memory*. Which is what the inter-text is." If I may borrow from Neil Badmington, "the internal coherence [of this book] lies in my approach . . . and not in the texts under consideration" (Neil Badmington, *The Afterlives of Roland Barthes* [London: Bloomsbury Academic, 2016], 5).

[21] Stafford, *Roland Barthes*, 97.

[22] Badmington, *Afterlives*, 8.

the Philippians, in conversation with Barthes, in order to analyze the writer as a text. Hence, the "texts" here are not only various works reconceived and read as such, but the writer of those works, one named, written as, "Paul." I agree with Marie Gil that Barthes's own writings "raised the possibility of reading a life 'as a text' and therefore of *writing* it,"[23] and I would suggest that the writer of letters later readers named "Romans," "1 and 2 Corinthians," and "Philippians" did likewise. In fact, part of the impetus for this book is that we too often read *against* the writer of these letters in our very efforts to understand him as an Author by molding the things he writes here and there to fit a body of work and a system of thought.[24]

Reading the aforementioned texts necessitates reading the readings of others. However, my goal when selecting secondary literature on these writings and their writer has not been to read exhaustively everything that has been said by interpreters of these materials, primarily because my interest is not to exegete them, to determine what they "really" meant or mean, to ascertain their Author's intention. Hence, my secondaries have been selected somewhat at random as, more often than not, they serve as arbitrary conversation partners, representative samples, illustrations of consensus, or of what Barthes referred to as the Doxa, by which he meant opinion, "nature," that which is "given." Even in the seemingly contrarian interpretations of scholars vis-à-vis those of "ordinary" readers, and in the recurring squabbles among scholars over age-old debates, there persist nonetheless certain tendencies, certain foundational assumptions, and a certain impulse toward systemization, for it is within a structure that "Paul" and his letters find habitation and become also habitable.[25] In *The Pleasure of the Text*, Barthes asks, concerning the work of critics, "How can we take pleasure in a *reported* pleasure . . . ? How can we read criticism?" His solution is to suggest that we recognize, attend to, and relish the nature of our relation to it. He answers, "Only one way: since I am here a second-degree reader, I must shift my position: instead of agreeing to be the confidant of this critical pleasure—a sure way to miss it—I can make myself its voyeur: I observe clandestinely

---

[23] Marie Gil, "Roland Barthes: Life as a Text," *Barthes Studies* 1 (2015): 35; emphasis in original.
[24] Cf. Badmington, *Afterlives*, 8: "[Barthes's] work offers not abstract philosophical propositions but careful, innovative *readings*. . . . If we forget this, if we look only for a body of theoretical work to master and summarize, we do Roland Barthes a profound disservice. We miss the point."
[25] See Barthes, *Lover's Discourse*, 45–47.

the pleasure of others, I enter perversion; the commentary then becomes in my eyes a text, a fiction, a fissured envelope."[26] My use of these materials is not motivated by an impulse to exploit them as foils or to manufacture straw men, but rather by a sort of fortuity and chance concomitance. They strike me as apposite intertexts, not only because they offer a perverse pleasure but also occasion an opportunity to identify moments of mythification among some writers and glints of what Barthes variously refers to in terms of drift, of the writerly, of the Neutral.

Not surprisingly, works of fiction have often done a particularly good job of refracting the conundrums of life-writing, whether it be biography or autobiography. The protagonist of Rabih Alameddine's novel, *An Unnecessary Woman*, exclaims, "Memory, memoir, autobiography—lies, lies, all lies."[27] Mark Dunn's *Ibid: A Life*[28] is another example. The novel's frame story, told through a series of letters exchanged between various characters, including the author who is a character in the book, is that of a biography, the sole manuscript of which has been lost, and for which only the endnotes remain. The author's publisher recommends publishing the endnotes by themselves. The author is conflicted: "I am quite torn over what to do. These notes, while extensive, are still, by definition, subordinate to the lost text—a text which I do not wish to invest another two years of my life attempting to reconstruct. While the notes illuminate the dusty, crepuscular corners of this man's life, they tell its story only through sidebar and discursion. The book, therefore, becomes a biography by inference."[29] He asks his brother, "Can the cloth of a man's life truly be defined by its embroidery?"[30] Ultimately, he decides to do it, and what follows is "a novel in footnotes." Similarly, Herman Wouk's *The Lawgiver*[31] is an epistolary novel told through letters, faxes, emails, texts, interoffice memos, and so on. The premise of the story is the conceptualization and production of a film depicting the life of Moses, but the novel *is* the life of Moses that Wouk wanted for so long to write, and in which he himself now features as a character. The novel tells the story of a failed story—a story never told and thus

[26] Barthes, *Pleasure*, 17; emphasis in original.
[27] Rabih Alameddine, *An Unnecessary Woman: A Novel* (New York: Grove Press, 2013), 127.
[28] Mark Dunn, *Ibid: A Life* (San Francisco: MacAdam/Cage, 2004).
[29] Dunn, *Ibid*, 5.
[30] Ibid., 6.
[31] Herman Wouk, *The Lawgiver: A Novel* (New York: Simon & Schuster, 2012).

nonexistent, and the novel life of its titular but absent protagonist, ultimately, a man of letters both real and figurative.[32]

Indeed, one sees the relation of life-writing to fiction even in the proliferation of terms used to refer to it. At its most basic, "life writing" is

> a broadly based term for all forms of writing about lives including biography, autobiography, diaries, which has been in use for the last thirty years. The term's inclusiveness acknowledges how hard it is to draw a rigid distinction between the different genres and how one genre may contain elements of another, a diary, for instance, being included within an autobiographical narrative, or an autobiographical discussion included in a biography.[33]

But Laura Marcus points out that the seemingly more narrowly focused concept of autobiography, itself already a neologism, "has been followed by a succession of new terms— 'autography,' 'autothanatography,' 'autobiografiction,' 'autofiction'—as if to express the hybrid and shape-changing qualities of a genre which sets out to represent the complexities of human life, experience, and memory."[34] In the end, I am not convinced that "autobiography" constitutes a genre at all, at least not in any strict sense. We encounter the *autobiographical* independent of any "autobiography." Such is an especially fitting way to approach the instances of self-narration one finds in the letters considered in this book. It is akin to Barthes's notion of the "novelistic," which gestures toward the self as fictional, dialogical, and textual. Barthes describes the novelistic as "another thing entirely [i.e., no plot, crisis, characters]: a simple unstructured contour, a dissemination of forms."[35]

---

[32] Other excellent examples include Jean-Paul Sartre, *Nausea*, trans. Lloyd Alexander (1938; Harmondsworth, Middlesex: Penguin, 1965); David Markson's *Wittgenstein's Mistress* (Champaign, IL: Dalkey Archive Press, 1988) and *Reader's Block* (Normal, IL: Dalkey Archive Press, 1996); A. S. Byatt, *Possession: A Romance* (New York: Random House, 1990); and Rabih Alameddine, *An Unnecessary Woman: A Novel* (New York: Grove Press, 2013). See also David Foster Wallace, "The Empty Plenum: David Markson's *Wittgenstein's Mistress*" in idem., *Both Flesh and Not: Essays* (New York: Back Bay Books, 2012), 73–116; Mikko Keskinen, "Blocks to, and Building Blocks of, Narrativity: Fragments, Anecdotes, and Narrative Lines in David Markson's Reader's Block," *Frontiers of Narrative Studies* 3 (2017): 224–37; and Roland Barthes, *The Preparation of the Novel: Lecture Courses and Seminars at the Collège de France (1978-1979 and 1979-1980)* (trans. Kate Briggs; New York: Columbia University Press, 2010).

[33] Linda R. Anderson, *Autobiography* (London: Routledge, 2001), 144.

[34] Laura Marcus, *Autobiography: A Very Short Introduction* (Oxford: Oxford University Press, 2018), 1.

[35] Barthes, *Pleasure*, 27.

As far as we know, the writer we refer to as Paul never wrote an autobiography or a memoir. We have never discovered any diary he kept. Moreover, considering the seemingly rather ambivalent and conflicted disposition he had with respect to the self, as we shall see, it is difficult to imagine that anyone will ever discover such a thing. Instead, the one we call Paul wrote letters. It seems pretty clear, or at least reasonable to believe, that he wrote more than are extant. Nevertheless, thirteen letters bearing his name appear in the New Testament as a result of having survived, having been saved, collected, and ultimately canonized, regarded as scripture and thereby deemed special, unique, authoritative, and, perhaps most of all, substantial, containing within them mysteries and an entire life in the most concentrated state. Although many readers take their ascribed authorship at face value, most scholars consider that only seven are "authentic" and then debate, with varying degrees of intensity, the authorship of the remaining six letters. To label these letters "authentic" is to say that they were actually written by Paul even though he most likely always did so with the assistance of an amanuensis, which already raises questions about what we mean when we say Paul is responsible for having written these letters.[36] Yet, despite this rather small body of work, subsequent writers have, with the help of curious if not problematic additional resources (e.g., the New Testament Acts of the Apostles, the so-called Deutero-Pauline letters, apocryphal works like *The Acts of Paul*, and so on), pieced together, woven, crafted a mind (if not an actual body), a life, an author, a man, an historical figure that has become the subject of countless and often very large biographies. To be sure, few identify themselves explicitly as biographies.[37] But

---

[36] Earle E. Ellis lists co-senders, secretaries, coauthors, letter recipients, and the authors of materials incorporated by Paul into his letters under the heading of "associates in writing" ("Coworkers, Paul and His," in *Dictionary of Paul and His Letters*, eds. Gerald F. Hawthorne, Ralph P. Martin, and Daniel G. Reid [IVP Academic, Downers Grove, IL, 1993], 188). Cf. Gregory P. Fewster, "'Can I Have Your Autograph?' On Thinking about Pauline Authorship and Pseudepigraphy," *Bulletin for the Study of Religion* 43/3 (2014): 30–39. I agree with Elsa Tamez who suggests that these seemingly silent partners played a rather substantive role. "Certainly Timothy is not simply a scribe; even though the rest of [Philippians] is written in the first person, Paul wants to make the coauthor official. As is common in these cases, Timothy would be conversing with Paul about the things he is writing, taking part in the content and form by clarifying points or expressing them in a better manner" ("Philippians," in Elsa Tamez, Cynthia Briggs Kittredge, Claire Colombo, and Alicia J. Batten, *Philippians, Colossians, Philemon* [Collegeville, MN: Liturgical Press, 2017], 37).

[37] It is tremendously difficult to determine precisely where to draw the lines of classification when so many works, both scholarly and popular, identify and speak about "Paul" variously in terms of his historical life, his thought, and his letters (as odd and arbitrary as such distinctions may seem to be). And the challenges of classification multiply once we add to the mix works in the area of reception studies, and works that attempt to de-center Paul such that the result is a sort of

behind each and every one persists an imagined figure, an Author, whose life is written herein and can be rewritten elsewhere.

We face a difficult predicament when we read Romans, 1 and 2 Corinthians, and Philippians (not to mention the other letters that bear a trace of one named Paul, or that are otherwise associated therewith). As letters, they read so clearly *as if* behind them there were one speaking directly and somehow, just maybe, even to us. As letters often are, especially between parties that share some sort of relationship other than purely bureaucratic or business, they are full of affect and emotion, asides, historical debris, names and signatures, ghosts of companions and contributors, and, most tantalizing of all, autobiographical snippets that seem to say so plainly, "this is me." There is an understandable desire to know this figure—the writing "I," the "I" that appears to inscribe itself—*as if* a person, an historical man, a subject. But to what end and at what cost? Given that these gestures toward the concrete are reality effects, are the "Pauls" of so many reconstructions identical with each other and the writer of these letters, or is "Paul" a signified and the letters ultimately signs and connotations? Does the name "Paul" serve only to anchor the letters, so to speak, and do we distill from them a "Paul," a name and a body that allow us to dispense with the letters, having transmuted them into individual works that coalesce into a corpus?[38] Perhaps there is no "Paul" but rather something else dispersed in and through the letters such that they are indispensable. According to Marie Gil, "Barthes's passion for biography is centered on

alternative biography, a counter-biography that is focused on the people he addresses directly or talks about indirectly in his letters and that construct "Paul" only secondarily in the reconstruction of those other individuals. But the classificatory problems only serve to further highlight what I want to address in this book. Naturally, biographies of Paul concern themselves with his life history (origins, heritage, education, occupation, career, founding of churches, imprisonments—always in terms of *where* rather than simply *that* he was imprisoned—even his physical appearance in some cases), his various "backgrounds" and "contexts" (Greek, Roman, Jewish, religious, ethnic), authentic versus inauthentic letters, the Paul of Acts versus the Paul of the letters, his "call," social status, chronologies, the "unity" versus "diversity" or "particularity" of his theology (i.e., vis-à-vis the various "occasions" of individual letters)—in a word, all the things that signify not actually a life but *life-writing, biography,* and in eminently reduced and reducible fashion, an accessible *essence,* an abstraction, to which the reader is now *introduced* as if the "Paul" thus (re)constructed were equally happy to meet her and to know her and be known by her, all in order that he and his work might be *understood.*

38 Cf. John Hamilton, *Philology of the Flesh* (Chicago: The University of Chicago Press, 2018), 6–7. Hamilton contrasts a "philology of the body" with a "philology of the flesh." The former renders written material in a manner that ultimately makes it gratuitous and redundant once its message is apprehended and its instrumental function is fulfilled, while the latter "exhibits a love that never wants to part with the word's material manifestation."

pleasure, it produces 'the pleasure of the text.'"[39] Returning then to our author, long dead both actually and metaphorically, perhaps all that is available to us is to quote, and to do so within the limitations imposed by the inevitable losses of history, and by the vagaries of curation, collection, and canonization. But leaving the writer to speak just as he is or does is problematic, if not impossible, and leads to dissatisfaction and denial. Therefore, hearkening to Barthes's call to refuse the readerly text in favor of the writerly, we might instead write in order to read, to effectively resurrect the dead author not by reinscribing his death through the repetition of words attached to the proper name but by interrupting and writing back to him, we free his words and our own through commentary that manhandles.

What frequently characterizes Barthes's work is an effort to peel apart things so closely and repeatedly associated that we have forgotten they were ever distinct and distinguishable in the first place, and then either to see what ideological function the firm and forgotten association (the Doxic connotation) serves, or to rewrite as text the thing independent of its associations. One sees this especially in *Mythologies* (i.e., early writings), though it is clearly at work in later writings like *Roland Barthes by Roland Barthes* and *A Lover's Discourse* also, as well as in the posthumously published notes from his lecture course on *The Neutral*.[40] Such is partly what I aim to do in this book: to resist connotation in favor of denotation; to refuse to equate the Author and the writer; and to relish the writerly over the readerly. Whereas the latter are marked by a sense of directness, transparency, and plainness whereby they seem to speak free of obstruction, the former are suffused with instability and permeated by fragmentation.[41] Because writerly texts are incomplete, therefore, their materiality is foregrounded and they allow for (if not insist on) "a perpetual present."[42] Writerly texts are precisely those that not only excite but also frustrate or irritate the reader, and that thereby resist both meaning and the desire for meaning.

---

[39] Gil, "Life as Text," 37.

[40] Roland Barthes, *The Neutral: Lecture Course at the Collège de France (1977-1978)*, trans. Rosalind E. Krauss and Denis Hollier (New York: Columbia University Press, 2005).

[41] George Aichele says of readerly texts, "They open themselves freely to the reader, seemingly withholding nothing . . . and satisfy her desire for meaning." In contrast, writerly texts are those that are constantly "provoking desires for but simultaneously withholding some satisfaction that they may never give" (*Simulating Jesus: Reality Effects in the Gospels* [London: Equinox, 2011], 71).

[42] Roland Barthes, *S/Z: An Essay*, trans. Richard Miller (1970; New York: Hill and Wang, 1974), 5.

Whereas many interpreters have regarded the more explicit autobiographical sections in the Pauline letters as having an apologetic function,[43] Beverly Gaventa shares George Lyons' critiques of this approach, which identifies in other autobiographical writings from the period a trend toward a concern for one's particular place in history,[44] and argues that "Paul's rhetorical approach, not his opponents reproaches, is responsible for the form in which he presents his 'autobiography.'"[45] What I suspect Lyons means to describe is a concern for one's (degree of) *significance* in history, and for (what the writer deems or desires as) the proper understanding of the individual in relation to history on the part of the audience. Autobiography functions as an attempt to exert control over circumstances and memory through narrativization.

Beverly Gaventa rightly notes the unwavering tendency on the part of those writing the history of earliest Christianity to take Galatians 1 and 2 as a playbook:

> Exegetes draw upon Gal 1:11-17 when they want to understand Paul's early life, his activity as a persecutor, or his calling. 1:18-1:24 offers a supplement to the travels of Paul as portrayed in Acts. 2:1-10 provides a source for the discussion of the Jerusalem council, and 2:11-14 supplies numerous possibilities for the reconstruction of the divisions within the earliest communities.[46]

For Gaventa, the result is a dissection: "Paul's personal narrative [is] divorced from his theological argument."[47] She cautions against such an approach saying, "If we habitually read a text only to learn about matters that exist outside it,

---

[43] Beverly Gaventa, "Galatians 1 and 2: Autobiography as Paradigm," in *NovT* 28 (1986): 309–26; Hans Dieter Betz (*Galatians: A Commentary on Paul's Letter to the Churches in Galatia* [Philadelphia: Fortress Press, 1979]) famously argued that Galatians was an apologetic letter written on Paul's own behalf.

[44] Gaventa, "Autobiography as Paradigm," 310, n. 1; citing George Lyons, *Pauline Autobiography: Toward a New Understanding* (Atlanta: Society of Biblical Literature, 1985), 26–73.

[45] Lyons, *Pauline Autobiography*, 8; Lyons provides an exceptional summary and critique of past approaches to the autobiographical statements in Galatians (75–121) and especially of so-called "mirror-reading" at the heart of such approaches (96–105), concluding that "'mirror reading' cannot provide a satisfactory answer to the question of the function of Paul's autobiographical remarks because it assumes precisely what must be established," namely "that Paul apologetically responded to charges in the form of a conclusion" (104–05). Cf. Nina Nikki, *Opponents and Identity in Philippians* (Leiden: Brill, 2019), 4; Nikki advocates for "controlled and detailed *mirror-reading*" because she contends that "whereas conventional polemic does not yield much historical information, non-conventional remarks . . . are more likely to reveal something historically significant."

[46] Gaventa, "Autobiography as Paradigm," 311–12.

[47] Ibid., 312.

then we lose sight of issues within the text that may be of equal importance. Indeed, we lose sight of the text altogether and read through it as if it were not there."[48]

One detects a sense of supplement in sorted assimilations of Paul's autobiographical vignettes, an effort to flesh out one thing or another, whether it be the life of Paul himself or some other thing with the help of his life. At the same time, we find ourselves engaged in contesting the meaning and ownership of a person's life, negotiating competing claims to that life story and to how it will be written in relation to whatever ideology is at issue. Barthes describes the insidiousness of description: "The language machine humming inside me . . . fabricates its chain of adjectives: I cover the other with adjectives, I string out his qualities, his *qualitas*."[49] Repeatedly, "Paul" is read as an example of some sort, whether that is how he is presenting himself, or interpreters are regarding him as such, or, most commonly and insidiously of all, as a combination of the two. Such is the consensus in one form or another. Barthes reflects on this problem in a fragment titled "Thus," which considers the inevitable frustration of constantly trying to define the other, the perpetual inadequacy of every description, and the unwavering desire for "a knowledge which would let him take the other *as he is*, thus and no other, exonerated from any adjective."[50] Of course, in our case, the Other, the Author, "Paul" cannot any longer simply be thus. He and the world in which he lived are reconstructions fabricated on the basis of what we perceive as traces and remainders we find in letters and other writings attributed or otherwise linked to him and that world. Hence, Barthes's ideal seems not only fitting but attractive: "And what would best resemble the loved being *as he is, thus and so*, would be the Text, to which I can add no adjective: which I delight in without having to decipher it."[51]

Returning to Gaventa, her thesis is that "Paul presents himself as an example of the working of the gospel."[52] But whether it is Paul's own life experience that informs and shapes his understanding of the gospel (à la F. F. Bruce and Seyoon

---

[48] Ibid., 312; cf. Hamilton, *Philology of Flesh*, 21: ". . . the philology of the flesh indulges in an oversaturation of meaning, which far outpaces the word's denotative functions. It demonstrates how we might disrupt the disruptions that bring language—our language—to a halt."

[49] Barthes, *Lover's Discourse*, 220.

[50] Ibid., 220; emphasis in original.

[51] Ibid., 222; emphasis in original.

[52] Gaventa, "Autobiography as Paradigm," 313.

Kim) or vice versa (à la Gaventa), there remains an intimate and inextricable connection between his "life" and his "thought." In nearly every case, interpreters (including Gaventa[53]) have read the self-narratives of the Pauline letters against the backdrop of Greco-Roman literary and rhetorical conventions, seeking to understand the *function* of autobiographical writing in its historical context. Self-narration is viewed as a device to be used by an author who is somehow known through these autobiographical remarks but also independently from them. Moreover, in nearly every case, the writer's autobiographical remarks are taken to be self-aware, transparent, cogent, and intentional (e.g., "I want to defend myself against criticism"; "I want to offer a model for imitation"; "I want my self to serve as a representative of some larger group"; etc.).

John Howard Schütz describes the story Paul tells of himself in Galatians as a "biography of reversal" that is fundamentally characterized by an antithetical quality wherein "Paul has set up a direct contradiction to the present by viewing his past as itself a negative mission directed against, rather than for, the Church."[54] Gaventa describes "the picture that emerges [as that] of an abrupt change from zealot for the Jewish tradition to zealot for the gospel," and argues that the most important thing to note here is "how Paul juxtaposes his former way of life with his response to revelation without explanation or elaboration."[55] Hence, the primary function of the "biography of reversal" is "to demonstrate that the singular gospel demanded of Paul an extraordinary and unequivocal response." This myth we attribute *to* Paul maps neatly onto the myth *of* Paul that is predominate among New Testament scholars.

Gaventa's conclusion is illuminating in the way that it exemplifies both the challenges one encounters in dealing with Paul's autobiographical vignettes and the general trends one discovers of those who have attempted to decipher them:

> Although the intensity of the tensions Paul is experiencing with the Galatians does not allow him to begin by offering himself explicitly as a paradigm

---

[53] Ibid., 322–26.

[54] John Howard Schütz, *Paul and the Anatomy of Apostolic Authority* (1975; Louisville: Westminster John Knox, 2007), 133. For Schütz, this "biography of reversal" is "the very essence of apostolic life," as Paul sees it (144); that is to say, Paul's life—both actual and written—functions as the concrete embodiment of "the gospel." Interestingly, in Schütz's reading, this is precisely where the articulation fails—or, depending on one's perspective, ultimately succeeds—insofar as Paul's "life" is non-repeatable (282–83).

[55] Gaventa, "Autobiography as Paradigm," 315.

of the gospel, he does do so indirectly. This paradigmatic dimension is accomplished by the repetition of the theme of the gospel's singularity, the inbreaking of revelation, and the insistence on the gospel's reversal of prior value-systems, all presented in the form of autobiographical material.[56]

The problem is that it seems the writer at once does and does not care about the self in the sense or manner that occupies so many modern readers. Consequently, he only ever writes about the self *in relation to* some other matter that appears to concern him. The challenge, therefore, at least in part, is to linger with a relational conceptualization of the self that recognizes the self as never anything but fluid and intersectional. Meanwhile, one can hear echoes of the interpretive inclinations one finds among various treatments of Paul's autobiographical statements: namely, exemplification (i.e., whereby Paul's narrated self functions as an example to be imitated), opposition (i.e., whereby the self is defined or determined by contrast to an imagined and narrated Other), and application (i.e., whereby the self is shaped in service to an end of some sort). Perhaps a better approach would be to resist and sidestep the urge to distill and decipher in favor of readings that attend to what are never anything more than traces and gestures of a writing-self that is peripheral, transient, and altogether inseparable from language.

Despite George Lyons' warning that "even if we remain ignorant as to the precise influences, what Paul says about himself and the way in which he says it must be understood within the context of antiquity and not on the basis of modern assumptions."[57] Fatima Tofighi's book, *Paul's Letters and the Construction of the European Self*[58] is but one recent book demonstrating the many complex and curious ways in which modern selves read Paul's self-narratives in relation to themselves and find themselves reflected back to them.

---

[56] Ibid., 326.
[57] Lyons, *Pauline Autobiography*, p. 7.
[58] Fatima Tofighi, *Paul's Letters and the Construction of the European Self* (London: Bloomsbury, 2017). The interpretive "fixations," as Tofighi calls them (xii), concern Christian responsibility toward civil authority in Romans 13, the rise and fall of "religion" in Europe vis-à-vis Galatians 2, and debates regarding gender in relation to Paul's discussion of veiling in 1 Corinthians 11. In Tofighi's estimation, each of these is a point where "Paul, who sometimes cannot fit in the framework of modern self-identification, through an interpretive twist, turns out to be the hero the moderns would identify with" (xii). Cf. Shoshana Felman, *What Does a Woman Want?: Reading and Sexual Difference* (Baltimore: Johns Hopkins University Press, 1993), 147 (cited in Anderson, *Autobiography*, 14): "That history subverts its witnessing and turns out to be linguistically involved with fiction does not prevent the fiction, however, from functioning historically and from having deadly factual and material consequences."

Hence, despite Lyons' assertion that "Paul's autobiographical remarks are fully intelligible when set in this context,"[59] my impulse throughout this book will be to leave them a little less intelligible.

With respect to matters of genre, form, and definition, what exactly counts as "autobiographical" discourse in the letters associated with Paul? Lyons defines autobiographical references in this context as "statements made by an author about himself which could be the basis for autobiography."[60] For Lyons, these include not only statements concerning the writer's past life, but also those addressing his present status and future plans. He contends that statements regarding future plans must be taken with caution "since future plans are contingent upon their completion."[61] But narrations of any past are no less contingent insofar as they are ineluctably determined by the exigencies and language of the present in which they are articulated. Not surprisingly, Lyon's definition also suggests that autobiography can be equated, more or less, with actual history. But the recounting of oneself and matters of one's life in a letter, and future plans especially, are premised upon desire, which is perhaps a more salient mark of the self than any historical actuality or "fact."

There are other problems with Lyons' definition. First, it would seem to imply that an author's own statements about himself enjoy a certain degree of privilege with respect to providing the foundation and authorization of any *biography* one might write about that individual. But in order for that to be the case, the writer would have to stand outside himself. And yet, when writing about oneself, one is forced to treat the subject as a character in a fiction, which means it is no longer any historical person being narrated but a simulacrum, which is in turn subject to the same array of narrative dynamics as any other storied figure. Second, it assumes a curious correspondence on the part of writer and reader concerning what counts as significant vis-à-vis the (life-)story. In other words, there is a sense that one already knows, or must know beforehand, the story in order to identify the facts pertinent to it. And it appears more often than not that the reader is the one most responsible for determining both the story and what autobiographical "facts" constitute it, which seems at odds with the idea that an historical person is directly

---

[59] Lyons, *Pauline Autobiography*, 7.
[60] Ibid., 9.
[61] Ibid., 9, n. 29.

and transparently communicating himself in and through autobiographical discourse.

Lyons later refines his definition a bit by saying that "autobiography may be identified as a description of a human life by the individual who live [*sic*] it, i.e., by a definition in terms of content not genre."[62] Hence, autobiography can take a wide variety of different forms, and Lyons ultimately suggests that autobiography is "a literary attitude."[63] Lyons cites Günther Bornkamm's claim that "despite their frequent personal references, Paul's letters 'are, of course, in no sense autobiography, but arose out of the apostle's work."[64] Thus, they are inescapably conditional and effectively inseparable from the writings that contain and circumscribe them. The situation we face is not altogether unlike the repeated references in Barthes's *Mourning Diary* to his work vis-à-vis both his mother's death and his mourning thereof. For example, in the entry from March 23, 1978, he writes:

> My haste (constantly verified in recent weeks) to regain the freedom (now rid of delays) of getting to work on the book about Photography, in other words, to integrate my suffering with my writing.
>
> Belief and, apparently, verification that writing transforms for me the various "stases" of affect, dialectizes my "crises."[65]

In the end, the use, form, and substance of autobiography is determined by the ends to which it is put. Paul's autobiographical statements "are characteristically intended to affect the reader's behavior—to accuse or defend, to persuade or dissuade, to praise or to blame."[66] Clearly, then, Paul did not write autobiography for its own sake: it is not a self-reflexive exercise

---

[62] Ibid., 17.

[63] Ibid., 20.

[64] Ibid., 22; Günther Bornkamm, *Paul*, trans. D. M. G. Stalker (New York: Harper & Row, 1971), xiv.

[65] Roland Barthes, *Mourning Diary: October 26, 1977—September 15, 1979*, trans. Richard Howard (New York: Hill & Wang, 2010), 105. The "book about Photography" refers to *Camera Lucida: Reflections on Photography*, trans. Richard Howard (New York: Hill & Wang, 1981), which is itself concerned as much with life-writing and self-narration as it is about anything having to do with photography. Barthes goes on to link his mythology on wrestling, his writings on Japan, his books, *On Racine* (trans. Richard Miller [1963; New York: Hill & Wang, 1964]) and *Lover's Discourse*, and his lecture course on "the Neutral" to various "stases" and "crises" and, most importantly, does so such that "writing" signifies differently than is customarily the case, especially among New Testament interpreters. (See n. 1 where the editor of *Mourning Diary* quotes Barthes description of the Neutral as "any inflection that avoids or thwarts meaning's paradigmatic, oppositional structure and consequently seeks suspension of the conflictual *données* of discourse.")

[66] Lyons, *Pauline Autobiography*, 24. The connection Lyons makes between the use of autobiography in ancient rhetoric (viz., epideictic) and the establishment of an orator's *ethos*, i.e., "his distinguishing

designed to explore his interiority or to better understand the nature of the self as such. This is all well and good, but what follows from this, however, is that the self is something to be deployed—an instrument to be used by the writer and thus independent of writing itself. Moreover, despite being aware of the fact that Paul is constructing his self only in relation to something or someone else, his autobiographical statements are taken to be accurate and representative. And even though they are only ever partial, conditional, and occasional, scholars take them cumulatively to capture a certain essence of their writer.

Admittedly, Lyons cautions contemporary readers against erecting historical realities on the basis of information gleaned from ancient narratives of the self because "the varied influences of rhetoric on the origins of autobiography serve as a reminder that truth is secondary to persuasion in its purposes. Contrary to the modern conception of biography and autobiography as subtypes of historiography, history was completely distinguished from both in antiquity in terms of origin, subject matter, and ideals."[67] Although upheld as an ideal, truth in ancient historiography was not objective and was subordinate to persuasive interests. The line between fact and fiction in both autobiography and biography was even more permeable.[68] The ethical import was not based on an obligation to the past but on an obligation to the edification and betterment of the reader who would find therein a model to be emulated.

However, there were limits to how far one could go, as well as constraints governing the suitability of autobiographical discourse. There was always a risk of impropriety whenever one wrote autobiographically in antiquity.[69] Self-description, especially used in service to providing a model for imitation, could be perceived as (if not actually be) self-flattery that, in turn, could be regarded as unethical or detrimental to the effectiveness of the rhetorical interests for which it is being employed. So there were qualifiers and restrictions imposed on it, and various techniques proposed to mitigate, curb, or circumvent its negative effects. Interpreters of Paul's autobiographical remarks regularly seek to demonstrate how he dutifully avoids these pitfalls. But in order to do so,

---

or customary moral character" (27), is arguably the cornerstone upon which most interpretations of Pauline autobiography are built (see 27–29).

[67] Ibid., 29.

[68] Ibid., 31.

[69] See ibid., 53–59.

interpreters must (i) presume to know the writer's intentions, (ii) presuppose that the autobiographical statements are relatively direct and transparent expressions through which he communicates his actual self, and (iii) occupy the position of the ideal reader as they imagine the writer to have imagined her. Moreover, this reading strategy is primarily grounded in the perpetuation of the myth of Paul wherein under the guise of discovering the historical Paul, interpreters ultimately manufacture a character that drives the plot of a much larger story.

What if we were to leave open the possibility that Paul's autobiographical remarks were scandalous? What if their potential to be perceived as unseemly and sordid was left untouched and allowed to stand? The point would not be to ascribe to the writer a subversive intent, which only repurposes the character for a story that seems different but that remains structurally the same. Rather, the aim would be to remain at the surface of the text and to linger with the materiality of the writing in order to untether text and reader alike. In addition, reading thus would resist and circumvent the urge to reconcile apparent inconsistencies and contradictions in favor of recognizing in their aggregate a rustling of the writing-self.

Lyons sides with Hans Dieter Betz in labeling Paul's self-narration as a "literary" problem because autobiographical discourse amounts to the author's rhetorical use of the self vis-à-vis the purposes of the various letters in which it occurs.[70] Paul's life, as narrated in Galatians and elsewhere, is the representation and embodiment of the gospel he promotes. I agree that it is a literary problem, but rather because the self is a fundamentally literary construct, and I am concerned here with both self-writing and the writing-self.

---

[70] Ibid., 73. Lyons ultimately turns his attention to 1 Thess. 1:2–3:13 noting differences in content but not so much in intent: "The autobiographical remarks . . . function parenetically to remind Paul's converts of the Christian ethical values they share, as embodied in the ethos of their *typos*. They are his imitators, but they, too, are examples" (221). For Lyons, it is the nature of Paul's relationships with the Galatians and the Thessalonians that account for the differences between the two autobiographical segments. I appreciate that there is a subtle difference between saying, on one hand, that the writer shapes the story of himself differently, or that he emphasizes different aspects of himself, based on the quality of relationship he has with his readers, and on the other hand, that he is engaged in a full-fledged apologetic. Nevertheless, notwithstanding Lyon's assertion that Paul introduces his past not out of any perceived necessity but of his own accord in order to present "his 'autobiography' as a paradigm of the gospel of Christian freedom which he seeks to persuade his readers to reaffirm in the face of the threat presented by the troublemakers" (171), there persists a conundrum: the presumption that a "real" and stable self independent of language lies behind the autobiographical expression, and yet that something exterior to that self mandates its expression and determines the shape of it.

As a literary problem, it lends itself especially well to a Barthesean mode of criticism—of *writing*—that is itself fundamentally literary.[71]

Philippe Lejeune defines autobiography as "a retrospective prose narrative produced by a real person concerning his own existence, focusing on his individual life, in particular on the development of his personality."[72] Laura Marcus notes two keys aspects in Lejeune's approach to autobiography: an emphasis on identity and a "pact" between author, text, and reader that promises and ensures veracity and authenticity. But we should also note in Lejeune's definition the terms "retrospective," "real person," and "development," which suggest that the writing-self occupies a privileged position that at once stands independently of its narration and benefits from a diachronic depth and progressive trajectory. But this image of stability and constancy is a chimera. Marcus rightly points out that "any narrative of the self and its life-story will entail a reconstruction, subject to the vagaries of memory, which renders the division between autobiography and fiction far from absolute."[73] According to Marie Gil, life should be read as a text because it "inverts the biographical doxa: life does not become a text, life is constituted as a text, it is a text in the process of becoming—we should say more precisely that its very substance is *the textual.*"[74]

Paul de Man's insistence that "autobiography . . . is not a genre or a mode, but a figure of reading or of understanding that occurs, to some degree, in all texts"[75] is particularly fitting for the self-narratives written not for their own sake but couched within letters, which by nature strike us as inherently autobiographical insofar as the first person is a natural function of the letter. "Most important of all for de Man," writes Linda Anderson, "is the problem that is encountered as soon as one attempts to make a distinction between fiction and autobiography, and finds oneself taken up in a whirligig of 'undecidability,' inhabiting a threshold between contradictory ideas."[76] Barthes championed contradiction. He relished amphibologies because, unlike the multiplicity of meaning that characterizes polysemy, their innate duplicity

---

[71] See, e.g., Stafford, *Roland Barthes*, 97–98, 108.
[72] Cited in Marcus, *Autobiography*, 3.
[73] Ibid., 4.
[74] Gil, "Life as a Text," 37; emphasis in original.
[75] Paul de Man, "Autobiography as De-facement," *Modern Language Notes* 94 (1979): 921.
[76] Anderson, *Autobiography*, 11.

offers up a different "fantasy" wherein one hears not everything but something else altogether.[77]

In Anderson's view, de Man sees autobiographical writing as an effort to endow the writer's "inscription within the text with all the attributes of a face in order to mask or conceal his own fictionalization or displacement by writing." This effort gives rise to a paradox: "The giving of a face, prosopopoeia, also names the disfigurement or defacement of the autobiographical subject through tropes. In the end there is only writing."[78] The inevitable naming through tropes evokes Barthes's frequent references to the image-repertoire throughout his autobiography. Although the fact that there is only writing appears to be a problem, a negative thing, a source of frustration, and a disappointment for de Man, Barthes clearly regards it as something possessing greater potentiality, positivity, and promise, an opportunity rather than an obstacle (though writing can be or function that way insofar as the writing subject is subjected to language) freeing writer and reader alike, as well as being a radical and revolutionary activity.

What is at the heart of this intrinsic paradox encountered in self-narration is that "autobiography always contains the epitaphic . . . it posits a face and a voice that speaks to us, as it were, beyond the grave."[79] In other words, autobiographical discourse does not present us with an historical reality, an Author who knows and can be known, but with a writer and a text wherein we brush up against, through drifts, gestures, and glints of writing, something irreducible, ephemeral, and unclassifiable. Autobiographical writing read through this lens opens up an avenue for the return of the author reimagined.

I do not mean to contend in this book that the writer of Romans, Corinthians, and Philippians consciously thinks of the self and of his self-narrations in this manner, even though I do think he may have imagined the self differently than we are accustomed to doing vis-à-vis both modern and poststructuralist notions of the self and self-narration. Rather, because I think this way about the self, I

---

[77] Barthes, *Roland Barthes*, 73. See also "The Rustle of Language" (in Barthes, *Rustle of Language*, 76–79 [1975]).

[78] Anderson, *Autobiography*, 12. "This is the dilemma of autobiography for de Man: to call up a figure for the self which is by the same token a 'disfiguring,' to depend for its 'life' on the same textual figure that contains the sign of its death: 'Autobiography veils a defacement of the mind of which it is itself the cause'" (ibid., 13, citing de Man, "Autobiography as De-Facement," 930).

[79] Ibid., 12.

read the writer's autobiographical *literature* in this manner. Although the writer of these letters writes about and refers to himself all over the place (recalling what was said above about the "I" being a literary function of the epistolary genre), this writer is typically reticent to discuss himself and the sorts of things commonly thought to constitute a life.[80] On the occasions when he does so, the narratives are terse, oblique, incomplete, and vague. I have not selected the self-narrative excerpts I read in the following chapters because I perceive them as more pregnant with history or meaning, or more transparent and concrete, or the best resources for accessing an author and his thought. Indeed, I take them to reflect the very opposite. As a result, these narratives problematize and destabilize the other instances of the "I" throughout the letters.

Many writers on Paul[81] are attuned to the fact that they have very little to work with in their attempts to reconstruct Paul's life and system of thought. Nevertheless, from these relatively minimal scraps of material they somehow reconstruct the substance of a life, replete with history, thought, feelings, character. All of this is enabled and reinforced "by a persistent, comforting myth, of a self-identical, self-knowing subject writing spontaneously and expressing a unified 'self.'"[82] But even in the case of a modern biography written about someone for whom there is a relative wealth of information available, there are some very real obstacles to life-writing. In the introductory chapter to his biography of Roland Barthes, Andy Stafford points out the obvious: If there are so many biographies of an individual (Paul, in our case), which of them is correct, and by what standard?[83] It almost goes without saying that biographies often, if not always, tell us more about the biographers than their subjects. We speak of (auto)biography as if it were a genre, but Stafford asks, "Is it history, literature,

---

[80] Gaventa, "Autobiography as Paradigm," 312; cf. Lyons, *Pauline Autobiography*, 9–16.

[81] I am trying hard to differentiate between someone writing on Paul and someone writing on say, Philippians, even though the two are rarely kept perfectly distinct on account of persistent notions of authorship and so forth.

[82] Sam Ferguson, *Diaries Real and Fictional in Twentieth-Century French Writing* (Oxford: Oxford University Press, 2018), 4.

[83] Stafford, *Phenomenon and Myth*, 3. Stafford references Sharon O'Brien who identifies four problems with biography: (i) "language is treated as a 'transparent medium capable of representing the world'"; (ii) "the character and the self are deemed 'knowable'"; (iii) "'the cause-and-effect linearity' of a chronological plot is considered 'a reliable way of ordering reality'"; and (iv) "the author is assumed to be 'a trustworthy narrator who understands the relationship between the private self and the public world'" (Sharon O'Brien, "Feminist Theory and Literary Biography," in *Contesting the Subject. Essays in the Postmodern Theory and Practice of Biography and Biographical Criticism*, ed. William H. Epstein [West Lafayette, IN: Purdue University Press, 1991]), 123–33.

fact, fiction or none of these? Does its generic status, and its parametrically defined methodology, depend on the subject, the object or the medium?"[84] And to these we could also add "reader." My aim here is not to write a biography of Paul. I am performing readings of select autobiographical statements of a writer. If anything, it is what David Ny refers to as an "anti-biography," which rejects the "conceptions of traditional biography—the notion that a linear, chronological, unified narrative can present us with an essential self."[85]

When the conversation turns to autobiography, added degrees of complexity arise. Rob Wilson identifies biography and autobiography as two chief factors in the process of "self-Americanizing dissemination" wherein writers represented America both in depicting it and in standing in for it, and points out that the "cultural rhetoric of American selfhood has been mapped in countless studies of American autobiography as a 'metaphorical' or 'prophetic' form of exemplary selfhood subsuming the agent as typical or 'typological.'"[86] In the end, "the production of the self *in* America gets identified *with* production of America as that space in which such exemplary selfhood is maximally possible."[87] Wilson suggests we treat autobiography as a "technology of the self" (à la Foucault) because it permits "individuals to effect by their own means or with the help of others a certain number of operations on their own bodies and souls, thought, conduct, and way of being, so as to transform themselves in order to attain a certain state of happiness, purity, wisdom, perfection, or immortality."[88] What Wilson describes here coincides once again with Barthes's desire for literary criticism that is itself *literary*. It is fitting, then, to focus on the writing and writerly "Paul" as a man of letters, a "paper person"[89] perpetually inscribed and reinscribed like a palimpsest by others, and to explore the perpetual transformations of the self into text, the writer's "translation" into the atopian paradise of writing.

---

[84] Stafford, *Phenomenon and Myth*, 220. Cf. Anderson, *Autobiography*, 13: "The pre-existing subject of autobiographical theory and its stabilization within a genre that could, like the self, be identified and recognized, was presented as an illusion, unmasked."

[85] O'Brien, "Feminist Theory and Literary Biography," 126.

[86] Rob Wilson, "Producing American Selves," in Epstein, ed., *Contesting the Subject*, 172.

[87] Ibid., 173.

[88] Ibid., 184, n. 2, citing Michel Foucault, "Technologies of the Self," in *Technologies of the Self: A Seminar with Michel Foucault*, eds. Luther H. Martin, Huck Gutman, and Patrick H. Hutton (Amherst: University of Massachusetts Press, 1988), 18.

[89] See Mieke Bal, *Narratology: Introduction to the Theory of Narrative*, 2nd ed. (Toronto: University of Toronto Press, 1997), 115–19.

Donna Haraway writes: "We are not immediately present to ourselves. Self-knowledge requires a semiotic-material technology to link meaning and bodies."[90] Language generally and autobiographical narratives in particular are two such semiotic-material technologies. But although much is inevitably lost in what such technologies produce, something else is potentially gained. It is the frayed edges of the roughly hewn self, especially in writing, that enable points of fusion with others that neither identify as the Other nor in any way possess the Other. "The split and contradictory self is the one who can interrogate positionings and be accountable. . . . The knowing self is partial in all its guises, never finished, whole, simply there and original; it is always constructed and stitched together imperfectly, and *therefore* able to join with another, to see together without claiming to be another."[91]

The starting point for Barthes's widely known essay, "The Death of the Author," is that "it is language which speaks, not the author."[92] One of the consequences of uncoupling and distancing the author is a fundamental collapse of time such that an author no longer *precedes* a work; rather "the modern writer (scriptor) is born simultaneously with his text; he is in no way supplied with a being which precedes or transcends his writing, he is in no way the subject of which his book is the predicate; there is no other time than that of the utterance, and every text is eternally written *here* and *now*."[93] And with the author's metaphorical and theoretical death comes also the death of any "theological meaning" that would act as a limit or capping off of meaning. Instead, the text is "a space of many dimensions, in which are wedded and contested various kinds of writing, no one of which is original: the text is a tissue of citations, resulting from the thousand sources of culture."[94] Our goal, the work of the critic, then, should no longer be to "decipher" the text but rather to distinguish and disentangle it.

> The space of the writing is to be traversed, not penetrated: writing ceaselessly posits meaning but always in order to evaporate it: it proceeds to a systematic

[90] Donna Haraway, "Situated Knowledges: The Science Question in Feminism and the Privilege of Partial Perspective," in *Feminist Theory Reader*, eds. Carole R. McCann and Seung-Kyung Kim, 4th ed. (New York: Routledge, 2017), 445.
[91] Ibid., 445.
[92] Roland Barthes, "The Death of the Author," in idem. *The Rustle of Language* (1968), 50.
[93] Ibid., 52; emphasis in original.
[94] Ibid., 53.

exemption of meaning. Thus literature (it would be better, henceforth, to say writing), by refusing to assign to the text (and to the world as text) a 'secret': that is, an ultimate meaning, liberates an activity which we might call counter-theological, properly revolutionary, for to refuse to arrest meaning is finally to refuse God and his hypostases, reason, science, the law.[95]

It is not difficult to see the ramifications of the author's metaphorical death and with it any terminal origin, source, or end to meaning for autobiography. The authorial and authorizing "I" in an autobiographical narrative is caught in an inescapable feedback loop. Hence, for Barthes, "linguistically, the author is nothing but the one who writes, just as *I* is nothing but the one who says I: language knows a 'subject,' not a 'person.'"[96] The masks or *personae* of the self are neither integrative nor additive. Instead, the self is the relation between the innumerable masks, and, because it neither precedes nor is ever fully finished, it is constantly being written and rewritten.

Time, memory, incompleteness, and inconclusiveness are in a complex and competitive relationship in self-narration. The contests between them are played out with and within the reader. "The problem with death when it is invoked rhetorically, as it frequently is within poststructuralist theory, is that it is never quite the end, and leaves space for all kinds of ghostly returns."[97] These ghosts emanate, in part, from the reader's desire and animate the writer. Indeed, Barthes wrote: "As an institution, the author is dead . . . but in the text, in a way, *I desire* the author: I need his figure (which is neither his representation nor his projection), as he needs mine."[98]

Whereas diaries are exceptionally diverse and frequently characterized by "a practice of recording the self in all its variation and instability, and by the renunciation of interpretation and synthesis,"[99] there is a palpable tension

---

[95] Ibid., 54.
[96] Ibid., 51.
[97] Anderson, *Autobiography*, 14.
[98] Barthes, *Pleasure*, 27; emphasis in original.
[99] Ferguson, *Diaries*, 19. Certain aspects of diaries thus performed resemble Hayden White's notion of history devoid of narrative (see "The Value of Narrativity in the Representation of Reality," *Critical Inquiry*, 7/1 [1980]: 5–27), and they are analogous also to Barthes's "novelistic" (i.e., the novel devoid of narrative; see, e.g., *How to Live Together: Novelistic Simulations of Some Everyday Spaces*, trans. Kate Briggs [New York: Columbia University Press, 2002]). Ferguson recognizes that diaries reflect a far greater range of form and purpose than what we ordinarily recognize as autobiography. Of particular relevance for this study, he includes lists among the many possible forms, and he notes that diaries are never perfectly successful in achieving their aims. His observation resonates with what Pontalis says in his autobiography when he notes that it is incomplete and unconcerned with

between part and whole in both autobiographical writing and writing about autobiography. J.-B. Pontalis writes: "I have adopted the idea that memory is mostly a fiction, my fiction for today. One shouldn't write *one* autobiography but ten of them because, while we have only one life, we have innumerable ways of recounting that life (to ourselves)."[100] Stafford, speaking of one of the more noticeable threads in Barthes's work, says: "There is a gap, a qualitative difference even, between the voice of a writer and the writer himself. It is not so much that language translates the writing-self, rather that the writer, and the voice of writing, are distinct activities, functions, and therefore value for the reader."[101] And Ferguson characterizes autobiographies in terms of their "totalizing attitude" marked by a "utopian aim of understanding the whole self."[102] Autobiographical writing is an attempt to give structure and, by extension, meaning to otherwise disparate occurrences through the processes of narrating and narrative shaping that typify it. There is an impulse toward selection and the creation of both a history and a plot. Self-narration appears to offer the writer a sense and semblance of stability.

Whether on the part of the writer or the reader, these notions of self-writing seem to presume, on some level or to some degree, a self that is already present and intact, prior to its articulation, waiting to be discovered, understood, and expressed. Much of what concerns me in this book is not merely the self being shaped *through* writing but also the very invention of the self in the act and moment *of* writing. My rationale is not only theoretical; I think it is also well-suited to the writer of the letters to the Romans, Corinthians, and Philippians who seems to imagine his self as anything but stable, durable, and enduring, and who also frequently distances himself from it, and, in various ways, is not especially interested in understanding it but instead devalues it—or rather strives to deflect connotations and significations that perpetually threaten to accrue to it.

Although there is no indication that Paul ever wrote an autobiography for its own sake or left behind a diary, scattered throughout the letters that bear

chronology: "'Auto,' certainly, but not 'biography:' an 'autography,'" if you like, a scripture of the self" (*Love of Beginnings*, trans. James Greene with Marie-Christine Réguis [1986; London: Free Association Books, 1993], xv).
[100] Pontalis, *Love of Beginnings*, xv.
[101] Stafford, *Roland Barthes*, 24.
[102] Ferguson, *Diaries*, 21 and 19, respectively.

his name are autobiographical vignettes, instances in which he narrates his self. We tend to accept these self-narrations at face value because we presume that the writer knows himself and his history and is able to speak directly and accurately about himself and his history. Furthermore, we tend to grant letters a degree of veracity that reinforces the reliability that we already ascribe to autobiographical narratives such that the two mutually vouch for one another. However, given that "fiction is a matter of degree rather than an all-or-nothing distinction,"[103] the autobiographical narratives we find in letters will bear the marks of fiction, not least of all in the various ways they attempt to code themselves as truth.

Letters occur frequently in ancient novelistic literature. Troy Troftgruben[104] has suggested that intradiegetic letters attest to the literary substance of a story by enhancing the sophistication, character, or weightiness of the narrative. Like written testimonies not about a person but about the story itself, they authenticate the narrative, generate empathy in the reader, and serve as generative actors in the events themselves. Arguably, the reason this works is that we make certain assumptions about actual letters, at least those we classify as personal letters. We tend to regard them as relatively transparent windows that provide us with more or less direct access to their writers. Then, having made such assumptions, we project those characteristics of transparency and accessibility onto the letters of fictional narratives. But narrative letters are no more real letters than literary characters are actual people. The verisimilitude that intradiegetic letters lend narratives is ultimately a type of reality effect. I think this, in turn, has implications for the way we read narratives—especially autobiographical narratives—embedded within actual letters.

Roland Barthes coined the term "reality effect" to identify the function of items or references in fictional works that appear fundamentally superfluous, "notations which no function (not even the most indirect) can justify."[105] Such notations most often occur in descriptions wherein "reality" presents itself and justifies its description by appeal to its self-evident nature. When a narrator includes such a notation in a story, it is to signify reality, to self-referentially

[103] Ibid., 29.
[104] Troy Troftgruben, "The Gravitas of Letters: Intra-diegetic Epistles in Jewish, Greek, and Christian Narratives." Annual Meeting of the Society of Biblical Literature, Ancient Fiction and Early Christian and Jewish Narrative Section. Atlanta, GA, November 2015.
[105] Roland Barthes, "The Reality Effect," in *The Rustle of Language*, 141.

highlight the narrator's "objectivity," and to limit flights of fancy by denoting the concrete. Barthes notes that while this is one thing in fiction, it is quite another in historical narrative wherein it becomes "the essential reference." Since historical narrative "is supposed to report 'what really happened,'" the question becomes: "What does the non-functionality of a detail matter ... once it denotes 'what took place?'" His answer is that "'concrete reality' becomes the sufficient justification for speaking."[106] Barthes's argument is that reality effects are rhetorical devices because ultimately reality effects do not in fact have *actual* reality as their referent, but the *concept of* reality as such. Despite appearing to denote reality, they provide the reader with something signifying the connotation of reality. This amounts to a collapse of the semiotic triangle of sign, signifier, and signified. "The 'concrete detail' is constituted by the *direct* collusion of a referent and a signifier,"[107] and the result is what Barthes calls the "referential illusion," which is the necessary condition for so much writing of history.

Much of history writing is marked by varying degrees of objectivity at the level of the discourse, which Barthes describes as "a special form of image-repertoire" that stems from the aforementioned referential illusion. Lacan referred to "the Imaginary" to indicate "the repertoire of imaginary identifications and mirror images through which the subject covers his relations with the external world in order to ameliorate its otherness."[108] Barthes borrowed this notion from Lacan and saw "the subject as diffracted through a mirror, identified with his own delusional reflected gaze."[109] In historical discourse, referents are often presented as if they speak for themselves; their very existence justifies their mention.[110] Autobiographical narratives present a particularly interesting case, for here the writer is also a participant in the things depicted. Occasionally, a third-person pronoun is used to indicate the past-tense actor who is now functioning as the present-tense narrator, but the words and actions depicted will inevitably conform to the characteristic mode of the position occupied by the narrator in relation to the things described: "The choice of the a-personal pronoun is merely a rhetorical alibi ...

---

[106] Ibid., 146.
[107] Ibid., 147.
[108] Anderson, *Autobiography*, 68.
[109] Ibid., 68.
[110] Barthes, "The Discourse of History," 132.

the true situation of the 'writer' is manifested in the choice of syntagms with which he surrounds his past actions."[111] For Barthes, "historical discourse does not follow the real, it merely signifies it, constantly repeating *this happened*." What we refer to as "the real" is ultimately nothing other than the meaning we have assigned to something after-the-fact.[112]

Narrative plays a fundamental role in the representations of reality one typical encounters in history writing. Hayden White states: "Arising, as Barthes says, between our experience of the world and our efforts to describe that experience in language, narrative 'ceaselessly substitutes meaning for the straightforward copy of the events recounted.' And it would follow that the absence of narrative capacity or a refusal of narrative indicates an absence or refusal of meaning itself."[113] Therefore, we tend to think there is a lot at stake if we fail to assimilate and account for every detail.

"Paul," as we "know" him, is an historical reconstruction that we all too seamlessly equate with a variety of implied authors inscribed within the letters bearing that proper name *and* deemed authentic—as opposed to letters labeled Deutero-Pauline, which also present implied authors that attempt to pose as the implied author of the authentic letters. "Paul" is thus a sort of fabrication, that is, not something wholly invented but certainly manufactured from bits of raw material and then molded and shaped to conform to some particular image, often unstated but always reflective of a cyborg-like hybridization: part "real" person, part ideal thing. The reconstruction anchors the letters and allows for the homogenization of the disparity among the implied authors of individual letters. To this assemblage we affix a proper name to combat the anonymity of the text.[114]

---

[111] Ibid., 133.

[112] Ibid., 139 and 140.

[113] Hayden White, *The Content of the Form: Narrative Discourse and Historical Representation* (Baltimore: The Johns Hopkins University Press, 1987), 1–2.

[114] I am referencing Roland Barthes, "Deliberation" (1979) in *Rustle of Language*, 369. Barthes frequently discussed the problematics, the ruse, the illusion of the proper name. See, e.g., "To Write: An Intransitive Verb," 20; "The Division of Languages," 114; "Cayrol and Erasure," 182 (speaking of the voice as a sign of the unnamed, "what is born or what remains of man if we take from him the materiality of his body"); and "Brecht and Discourse," 218–19. On "Paul" as an implied author, see especially Janice Capel Anderson, "Matthew, Mark, and Paul: The Vintage Sounds of the Implied Author," in *Bible and Theory: Essays in Honor of Stephen D. Moore*, eds. Jason Coker and Scott S. Elliott (Lanham, MD: Lexington Books/Fortress Academic, 2020). See also Fewster, "'Can I Have Your Autograph?'"

Ultimately, there will be no "Paul" in this book. I will resist the urge, as often as possible, even to allow the name to serve as a representative placeholder, lest it become a cipher for an Author, an originator and owner of ideas, a man that can be known and understood if not almost touched. Because it is precisely at that point where a curious and problematic shift takes place, a slippage. Were the historicizations of Paul to cease with contextual reconstruction and appreciation of his ordinariness, then we might be in a better position to more productively focus either on the writings associated with him independently of the ascription of genius or the production of "Paul" after the fact through reception and ideology. But instead the reconstructions serve ideological interests by setting Paul and his ideas in sharp relief so that he emerges as a unique specimen, an unrepeatable singularity. As we shall see, this too serves ideological interests insofar as Paul becomes the inimitable thing that is somehow to be imitated. For too long, biblical scholarship has perpetuated a problematic and ideologically suspect mode of criticism in which "a work," such as a letter of Paul, for example, is "often but a pretext in which the author of a work, reconstructed by way of psychology, sociology, philosophy or metaphysics, [is] given a particular image," and "made . . . into a kind of gospel, in which no word or piece of punctuation [is] rejected as pure chance, play or irony, and in which the author [is] deemed to have meant exactly what was said."[115] The force of "gospel" here is compounded by the fact that the letters of Paul are nothing short of *scripture*. Even to those who profess no religious or theological allegiance to the Bible, the letters ascribed to Paul are still often treated with a kind of religious fervor. They are granted a sacred status insofar as they are like a holy chalice *containing* the ideas of their author, and they function as keys by which to unlock the mysteries of his thought and thus of his very self.

For Roland Barthes the way out of this problematic conundrum, this myth, is writing—not "the work" or the product, but the act of writing on the part of both the writer and the critic. An important and virtually constant refrain throughout Barthes's own writings is "how logothetical status was dependent on the modern critic . . . rather than inherent in the text,"[116] and he justified his literary mode of literary criticism on political and ethical grounds. The risk with a book like this is that it inadvertently, despite itself, perpetuates through

[115] Stafford, *Phenomenon and Myth*, 93.
[116] Ibid., 173.

inversion the very myth I aim to trouble and unravel. Nevertheless, the goal is first to identify texts of bliss in the instances of self-narration throughout these letters through the performance of close (re-)readings and rewritings of them in conversation with Barthes, their writer, and other readers and intertexts. In the course of doing so, I want to treat these letters as writerly texts, rather than as the readerly works they have become, by identifying moments in them where I find what Barthes refers to as "twinklings" of the Neutral, to write with the writer those gestures of the self that emerge amid "rustling."

Therefore, instead of the proper name, here there is only a writer—perhaps even writers, because the writing and writerly self is always fragmented and plural—and specifically a writer of letters. There are thirteen letters in the New Testament that bear the name "Paul" as their sender. On the basis of content and style, scholars customarily distinguish between "authentic" letters of Paul (viz., Romans, 1 and 2 Corinthians, Galatians, Philippians, 1 Thessalonians, and Philemon) and the non-Pauline or Deutero-Pauline letters (Ephesians, Colossians, 2 Thessalonians, 1 and 2 Timothy, and Titus). Two rather obvious problems emerge. First, who among us actually imagines that someone would know us, ascertain our "essence," from, say, seven random emails, even very lengthy and substantive emails, that just happen to have survived the vicissitudes of history, regardless of whether it was due to sheer chance or to the varied and ever-changing and aggregating reasons, whether expressed or subconscious, of assorted audiences, whether intended or not? Furthermore, there is a circularity inherent in the foundation upon which all of this is built: this collection enables scholars to identify a common writer, who is an author named "Paul," and it does so because they see the hand and the mind of this author reflected in these "works." But even if we go so far as to grant that imitations of Paul (e.g., in the Deutero-Pauline letters) betray the presence of an impostor, all that remains is difference. To move from there to an identification of the anterior with the original and actual "Paul" and then to presume that we have come to *know* this *person* to whatever extent is to perform a shift from one operation of signification to a second-order operation of signification; it is to leap from history to myth.

The same issue lies at the heart of both problems. It is not that the self is an essence so mysterious, complex, impenetrable, etc. that it cannot be reached or fully captured, as if it were the case that if only we had even *more* letters

then we would reach our goal, the fully revealed and transparent "Paul."
Nor is it that we do not identify threads of similarity. With respect to the
latter, though, the aforementioned circularity makes it nearly impossible to
determine if the similarity emerges from the letters or is a preexisting filter
through which we read the letters such that the latter serve only to confirm the
image of our prefabricated author. Moreover, a lot of ideological machinery
is at work in determining the limits of similarity when deciding which letters
will be "authentic" or "inauthentic." And, finally, where is the imagined author
once we factor in quotation, allusion, and the role played by an amanuensis in
the actual writing—the material production—of the letter? Or what of missing
letters alluded to in the ones we have, the compiling and editing of composite
letters, collecting, eventually canonizing, and even translating—and thus
recontextualizing and shifting the audiences—of these otherwise "occasional"
acts of writing? The issue, rather, is that the self is a fiction that requires and
exists within a space of perpetual writing and rewriting.

At the heart of Barthes's "autobiography," *Roland Barthes*, is a fundamental
resistance to the self as something both essential and coherent that persists
through time and articulation, which can therefore be expressed in and
through language. The book reflects not simply a resistance to *his* self but to *the*
self. I see in the self-narrative moments scattered about the letters attributed
to the writer, Paul, a similar resistance. Michael Bird rightly observes that Paul
did not consider his Jewishness as the core of his identity.[117] Bird does a fine
job of demonstrating that Paul considered his identity to be located squarely
in the new epoch of Christ. However, Bird's recognition of this alternative
identity notwithstanding, what remains insufficiently problematized in Bird's
study and those of so many others on the topic is the writer's understanding
of identity in the first place. Like Barthes, the writer of the New Testament
letters we assign to Paul signals a desire to reconcile human understanding
and reality.[118] Diana Knight points out that, in Barthes's essay on the Eiffel
Tower in *Mythologies*, it is "its very uselessness [that] is essential to its utopian
potential."[119] Matt Waggoner recognizes something similar in the work of

---

[117] Michael Bird, *An Anomalous Jew: Paul among Jews, Greeks, and Romans* (Grand Rapids: Eerdmans, 2016), see 5–8.
[118] Cf. Diana Knight, *Barthes and Utopia: Space, Travel, Writing* (Oxford: Clarendon Press, 1997), 57.
[119] Ibid., 59.

Theodor Adorno: "There is something utopian about obsolescence in a society in which relations between people are governed only by the value of utility, which is why 'tenderness between people is nothing other than awareness of the possibility of relations without purpose.'"[120] Barthes himself says that "it is the text's very uselessness that is useful."[121] Hence, Sontag explains, "The characteristic point of Barthes's arguments-by-paradox is to vindicate subjects untrammeled by utility."[122] Knight goes on to describe the Eiffel Tower in Barthes's "mythology" as "basically a degree zero moment, an empty signifier which attracts secondary meanings like a lightning conductor—meanings extracted by human beings 'from their knowledge, their dreams, their history.'"[123] I contend that "Paul" is akin to Barthes's Eiffel Tower in two ironically opposing ways. On one hand, he writes about the self in a somewhat similar fashion, suggesting that it (or the subject, or at least the name) functions ultimately as an empty signifier. On the other hand, the history of Paul's reception is such that he himself functions as an empty signifier, a cipher on and through which are melded countless secondary meanings drawn from knowledge, dreams, and history—all the makings of the image-repertoire.

One of Barthes's most direct statements on the image-repertoire occurs in *A Lover's Discourse*:

> The Image-repertoire is precisely defined by its coalescence (its adhesiveness), or again: its power of association: nothing in the image can be forgotten; an exhausting memory forbids voluntarily escaping love; in short, forbids inhabiting it discreetly, reasonably. I can certainly imagine procedures to obtain circumscription of my pleasures (converting the scarcity of frequentation into the luxury of the relation, in the Epicurean fashion; or again, considering the other as lost and henceforth enjoying, each time the other returns, the relief of a resurrection), but it is a waste of effort: the amorous glue is indissoluble; one must either submit or cut loose: accommodation is impossible (love is neither dialectical nor reformist).[124]

---

[120] Matt Waggoner, *Unhoused: Adorno and the Problem of Dwelling* (New York: Columbia University Press, 2018), 82.

[121] Barthes, *Pleasure*, 24.

[122] Susan Sontag, "Writing Itself: On Roland Barthes," in *A Roland Barthes Reader*, ed. Susan Sontag (1982; New York: Barnes & Noble, 2009), xxi.

[123] Knight, *Barthes and Utopia*, 59; citing Roland Barthes, *The Eiffel Tower and Other Mythologies*, trans. Richard Howard (New York: Hill & Wang, 1979), 5; cf. Sontag, "Writing Itself," xxi: "it is the uselessness of the Eiffel Tower that makes it infinitely useful as a sign, just as the uselessness of genuine literature is what makes it morally useful."

[124] Barthes, *Lover's Discourse*, 51.

It is the image-repertoire rather than any internal cohesion, which comes from outside through the eye of reader-observer, that provides the self with the illusion of wholeness; and it is a product, a mark, of desire. In *Camera Lucida*, Barthes writes: "In terms of image-repertoire, the Photographer (the one I intend) represents that very subtle moment when, to tell the truth, I am neither subject nor object but a subject who feels he is becoming an object: I then experience a micro-version of death."[125] The image-repertoire is that which provides the setting, plot, dialogue, networks of associations, historical material, and fodder of the writer's life reflected and refracted back to himself. It is at once necessary, inescapable, immutable, and problematic. Anderson describes *Camera Lucida* as a book in which Barthes "returns to the problems of the autobiographical but with a sense of urgency and almost overwhelming pain."[126] Written in the wake of his mother's death, the book revisits photography "as a different kind of representational space where questions of essence, which are treated as fallacious within writing where meaning is plural and substitutive, can again be raised."[127] In referring to a particular photo of his mother, for example, Barthes speaks of how it is an impossible image insofar as it represents her (and himself) to him in a way he could never have experienced or known her by virtue of his retrospective viewpoint.

At the same time, however, each photograph contains within it a punctum: a glimmer of something that lives beyond the image. The punctum is often an "unnecessary" or unplanned, "irrelevant" detail. The punctum is "a piercing, uncodifiable detail that can pass from photograph to viewer and which is powerful enough to connect the spectator again with the 'real' of the past."[128] For Barthes, photographs have greater potential to overcome limits or barriers to the "real" that texts cannot escape. I think, however, there are punctum-like aspects of texts, instances in which language is subverted and the unassimilable bleeds through, hovering on the surface of the text.[129] These are the traces of a writer in writing. The "Paul" we identify as the "Author" behind a body of work, of whose "thought" we speak," whose "life" we imagine and write, whose model we erect and emulate, is a chimera; "he" is a series of textual effects. But

---

[125] Barthes, *Camera Lucida*, 14.
[126] Anderson, *Autobiography*, 71.
[127] Ibid., 71.
[128] Ibid., 72.
[129] See, e.g., what Barthes says concerning typos: "faults of essence . . . the typo is never vague, *indecipherable*, but a legible mistake, a meaning" (*Roland Barthes*, 97; emphasis in original).

at the level of the writing—not behind or beneath it— and across the letters, there is a writer that rustles.

Barthes strongly resisted the impulse toward "totalising commentary,"[130] which perverts writing. In *S/Z*, he contends that the aim of criticism and commentary should be to "manhandle" and "interrupt" the text, and thereby to operate against an ideology of totality.[131] Such is the goal of this study. What I find in the self-narratives peppered throughout the letters ascribed to Paul is not a window into the thought or lived experience of an historical person. Instead, I find on the part of a writer the desire for a structure because it is inhabitable even as he resists that structure specifically as well as structuration generally.[132] And that desire is marked by "the cutting up of a period, of a work, into phases of development," which, despite being "a purely imaginary operation," grants the writer access to a "game of intellectual communication" in which he makes himself intelligible.[133] But the writer's efforts to make himself intelligible (whether to others or to himself) is not perfectly in sync with our efforts to do likewise with him. Hayden White notes, for example, that "the value of narrativity in the representation of real events arises out of a desire to have real events display the coherence, integrity, fullness, and closure of an image of life that is and can only be imaginary."[134]

---

[130] See Stafford, *Phenomenon and Myth*, 200. Barthes was enamored of the way Bertolt Brecht's work opposed the "myth of unity" that characterizes ideology.

[131] Barthes, *S/Z*, 15.

[132] See Barthes, *Lover's Discourse*, 46, and *Roland Barthes*, 119.

[133] Barthes, *Roland Barthes*, 145.

[134] White, *Content of the Form*, 24.

2

The Rustle of Paul

Romans 7:14-25 is the most controversial and complicated instance of self-narration in Paul's *oeuvre*. Here, Paul performs what is at once both autobiography (of a sort) and a rhetorical speech-in-character. Paul writes himself as a character that is at once also the narrator. As such, the pericope intertwines and embodies narrative discourse, history, autobiography, represented speech, and complex focalization. And by positioning Paul as a character-narrator, it in turn renders his reliability unstable. I begin with this passage precisely because it is rarely, if ever, accepted as truly autobiographical by professional interpreters. Therefore, my treatment of this passage is intended to problematize all autobiographical statements in Paul's letters and to frame my readings of other Pauline instances of self-narration in subsequent chapters.

Most scholars agree that Romans is the only letter Paul wrote to recipients he either did not know personally or who at least were not part of a congregation that he himself founded. It may have served as a letter of introduction in anticipation of his arrival. Hence, it may have acted as a self-inscribed—an *auto-graphed*, if you will—letter of recommendation wherein the writer vouches for Paul. Near the middle of the letter, we encounter one of the more convoluted and theoretically interesting pieces of self-narration in the Pauline corpus. It is no surprise that the secondary literature on the passage is immense, and it is interesting how much of that literature is devoted to correcting what would seem to be the "obvious" or "natural" reading, especially when both ordinary and academic readers alike ultimately reproduce the same subject, or at least the same sort of subject, at a fundamental level. Taken at face value, one would be inclined to regard the first-person pronoun running throughout vv. 7–25 as an accurate and reliable reflection of the writer, who is caught in an ongoing struggle between duty and desire. This particular Paul is an "everyman" in his battle against "the flesh" and a paragon of one who strives for excellence and perfection in his obedience to the Law of God in his inmost self.

However, since the publication of Krister Stendahl's article, "The Apostle Paul and the Introspective Conscience of the West,"[1] biblical exegetes argue that were the author speaking of such an internal struggle it would contradict autobiographical statements of Paul elsewhere in his letters, not least of all Phil. 3:4b-6 where Paul boasts of his Jewish heritage and of his ability to be righteous under the Law, even going so far as to describe his performance as "blameless." For example, Ben Witherington states, "There is not a shred of evidence that Rom. 7.14-25 describes Paul's mental outlook prior to his conversion to Christianity, and as Philippians 3 suggests, it hardly describes his views as a Christian looking back on his Jewish past."[2] Furthermore, exegetes contend, if taken as indicative of Paul's present state, the passage also seems to contradict the argument of Romans 7 as a whole, which is concerned with defending the Law against the charge of being morally flawed because it arouses sinful passions, and with the relevance of the Law in relation to the situation facing the Christian congregation in Rome.

The decisions that interpreters make regarding what constitutes or counts as reliable information (e.g., privileging the "facts" of Phil. 3:4b-6 over the "performance" of Rom. 7:14-25, especially when one considers the tendency of so many "ordinary" readers to identify with the latter while overlooking the former altogether) are driven by fundamentally theological concerns.[3] Philippians is a check against Romans not because it is ultimately any less of a performance but because a certain positioning of Paul requires it. R. Barry Matlock summarizes the situation this way:

> We might describe the [New Perspective] as resting on two "pillars," two fundamental axioms: that Paul was not really about individual sin, guilt and forgiveness, but rather that communal and social concerns to do

---

[1] Krister Stendahl, "The Apostle Paul and the Introspective Conscience of the West," *HTR* 56 (1963): 199–215.

[2] Ben Witherington, *Paul's Letter to the Romans: A Socio-Rhetorical Commentary* (Grand Rapids: Eerdmans, 2011), 201.

[3] R. Barry Matlock, "Almost Cultural Studies? Reflections on the 'New Perspective' on Paul," in *Biblical Studies/Cultural Studies: The Third Sheffield Colloquium*, eds. J. Cheryl Exum and Stephen D. Moore (Sheffield: Sheffield Academic Press, 1998), 433–59. Cf. Richard A. Horsley, ed., *Paul and Empire: Religion and Power in Roman Imperial* (Harrisburg, PA: Trinity Press International, 1997), 5–7; James G. Crossley, *Reading the New Testament: Contemporary Approaches* (London: Routledge, 2010), 86–96.

with Jewish and Gentile relations, practical concerns arising from Paul's mission, were his primary context and focus; and that the Judaism of Paul's day was not a "legalistic" religion of meritorious "works-righteousness," so that Paul's "opponents," and his position over against them, must be reassured.[4]

Matlock identifies in the New Perspective what he calls a "residual biblicism," by which he means "the apparent desire to have Paul affirm our own deepest values, to find ready to hand in this biblical witness that which we may now affirm for ourselves."[5] He ultimately asks whether we could ever tell a story of Paul without it being a thinly veiled rendering of our own.[6] Perhaps instead of reading Romans 7 in the light of Philippians 3, we would be better off reading Philippians 3 in the light of 1 Corinthians 9, recognizing that the figure of Paul remains as pliable as ever and continues to "become all things to all people." My point is not to argue against the New Perspective per se, nor is it necessarily to contend that Paul was plagued by guilt. My concern is the use of the letters and the overarching conceptualization of them—that is, what they are vis-à-vis the writer.

The situation is similar to what the reader encounters in Gal. 2:18-20 where it is also unclear whether the *ego* refers to the writer specifically or functions as a cipher for every individual believer.[7] If not disregarded as autobiography altogether, the writer's words here are taken as quasi-autobiographical, as something possessing merely the (semi-formal) appearance of autobiography because it suits a rhetorical function oriented toward serving either as an anonymous or generic example or case study or as an identification on the part of certain readers who "relate to" what is being said, who see themselves in the characterological words of the writer. Hence, George Lyons states that "in some instances Paul's 'I' has been understood to be nearly equivalent to

---

[4] Ibid., 435.
[5] Ibid., 442.
[6] Ibid., 449. The writer can only ever be known to himself through his image-repertoire and the Author, in turn, can only be known through our own that enfolds the former, and both are inevitably and inescapably out-of-sync and in friction with each other. See also, Johnson-DeBaufre, "Narrative, Multiplicity, and the Letters of Paul"; Melanie Johnson-DeBaufre and Laura S. Nasrallah, "Beyond the Heroic Paul: Toward a Feminist and Decolonizing Approach to the Letters of Paul," in *The Colonized Apostle: Paul through Postcolonial Eyes*, ed. Christopher D. Stanley (Minneapolis: Fortress Press, 2011), 161–74.
[7] See Gaventa, "Autobiography as Paradigm," 318. Gaventa references C. E. B. Cranfield, *Romans* (Edinburgh: T&T Clark, 1975) 1:342–47 for a summary of the various positions on this figure's identity and/or function.

'anyone,' and thus not strictly autobiographical," and references Rom. 7:7-25 as "the most difficult example of this anthropological 'I.'"[8] Regarding the situation in Galatians, Gaventa writes:

> The difficulty in separating the general from the individual here is indicative of their interrelationship in the larger argument. Paul does not intend the first-person singular here or earlier simply to refer to "one." Nor does he speak of his own experience in order merely to defend his apostolate or to boast of his relationship to Christ. Instead, he sees in his experience a paradigm of the singularity of the gospel, and he uses his experience to call the Galatians into that singularity in their own faith-lives.[9]

Ever since Stanley K. Stowers set out his arguments for reading Romans 7 as an instance of speech-in-character (*prosopopoeia*), "a rhetorical and literary technique in which the speaker produces speech that represents not himself or herself but another person or type of character,"[10] interpreters have effectively shifted their attention from identifying the implied author to identifying the implied character in their effort to solve the perceived problem of the writer's use of the first-person pronoun. Some of the more intriguing possibilities are those put forward by Mark Seifrid,[11] Jan Lambrecht,[12] Robert Jewett,[13] and Nicholas Elder.[14] Seifrid suggests that Paul "here portrays himself according to a pattern found in early Jewish penitential prayer and confession from the limited perspective of his intrinsic soteriological resources."[15] Such prayers "represent the penitent(s) from a limited perspective determined by group or personal guilt, while acknowledging that a broader framework exists, which is dependent upon divine mercies."[16] In this instance, the writer is a representative who stands in solidarity with those he represents.

Lambrecht, meanwhile, sees in Rom. 7:14-25 a rhetorical "I" that functions to depict Paul's pre-Christian situation from the perspective

---

[8]   Lyons, *Pauline Autobiography*, 10. It is not clear what "strictly autobiographical" means, given the diversity of forms that it can take. Poststructuralist theory only complicates this even further.

[9]   Gaventa, "Autobiography as Paradigm," 318.

[10]   Stanley K. Stowers, *A Rereading of Romans: Justice, Jews, and Gentiles* (New Haven: Yale University Press, 1994), 16–17; see also 264–84.

[11]   Mark A. Seifrid, "The Subject of Rom 7:14-25," *NovT* 34 (1992): 313–33.

[12]   Jan Lambrecht, *The Wretched "I" and Its Liberation: Paul in Romans 7 and 8* (Grand Rapids: Eerdmans, 1992).

[13]   Robert Jewett, *Romans* (Minneapolis: Fortress Press, 2007).

[14]   Nicholas Elder, "'Wretch I Am!' Eve's Tragic Speech-in-Character in Romans 7:7-25," *JBL* 137 (2018): 743–63.

[15]   Seifrid, "The Subject of Rom 7:14-25," 320.

[16]   Ibid., 322.

of his post-conversion life as a Christian. According to Lambrecht, "Paul re-reads the past through the prism of faith."[17] In this case, the writer not only represents an Other, but an Other that is still himself at another time, a past interpreted, assessed, and fundamentally shaped by a later time that is not perfectly distinct but exists within the wake of the past it is actively (re)inventing.

Building on Lambrecht, Jewett highlights the affective purpose of *prosopopoeia*: "An imaginary person or type is allowed to speak in the first person in order to make an emotionally effective argument."[18] Elder furthers this affective dimension and builds on the proposal of Austin Busch[19] to argue that the writer's use of the first-person pronoun is a cipher for the character of Eve (i.e., rather than Adam as any number of other interpreters have suggested) who has been cast here as "a popular tragic subject: the lamenting, morally torn woman."[20] Elder demonstrates the ways in which the writer of Romans has woven Jewish traditions concerning Eve from the Second Temple period (viz. from *Sirach*, *2 Baruch*, Philo, *The Life of Adam and Eve*) together with the trope of female lament from Greek tragedy. In Elder's view, the character of Eve serves the writer's argument because she is the epitome of an Aristotelian tragic figure insofar as her fate is something that befalls her rather than something that results from anything innate within her, the proliferation of her grief fulfills the prediction of Gen. 3:16, and she is the counterpart to Adam who is central to the writer's argument in Romans 5. Ultimately, the writer performs a speech-in-character as Eve in Romans 7 for pedagogical reasons. "The protoplasts' joint culpability, however, is not the end of the story for Paul. He addresses Eve in Rom. 8:1-2, indicating that the consequences of her error are apocalyptically undone. If, as Aristotle suggests, the purpose of tragic lament is to provoke pity or fear, the purpose of this provocation is for the cathartic release of these emotions in the audience itself. By addressing Eve

---

[17] Lambrecht, *The Wretched "I"*, 90; cited in Jewett, *Romans*, p. 443.

[18] Jewett, *Romans*, 443. Commenting on an example of *prosopopoeia* in Epictetus, Jewett writes, "Whether the anecdote is true or not is less relevant for the argument than the argumentative point itself" (444). To support this point, Jewett offers another example from Epictetus concerning a robbery. Evidence suggests that the robbery did indeed happen, but "Epictetus's use of this element of *prosopopoeia* serves to substantiate a philosophical argument that in and of itself had nothing in common with thievery" (444).

[19] Austin Busch, "The Figure of Eve in Romans 7:5–25," *BibInt* 12 (2004): 1–36.

[20] Elder, "Wretch I Am!," 748.

and assuring her that she now has no condemnation, Paul provokes a cathartic release of the pity the audience felt for Eve and for themselves."[21]

Such is the consensus reading: the 'I' of Romans 7 is a script. This reading occupies the realm of *Doxa*: "Broadly speaking, however, all that is considered true, or at least probable, by a majority of people endowed with reason, or by a specific social group, can be called doxic."[22] In Barthes's work, the doxic characterizes and enables the readerly text with its tendency to affirm, to leave the reader "with no more than the poor freedom either to accept or reject the text" and to make reading "nothing more than a *referendum*," as opposed to the writerly text that moves the reader from a consumer of the text to its producer.[23]

Admittedly, reading Rom. 7:14-25 as a speech-in-character does not actually settle the issue of who the "I" actually *is*, but that is in fact secondary to the work it does do, which is to make clear who the "I" is *not*—namely, Paul. According to Jewett, "Paul's speech-in-character is artificially constructed in the light of his preconversion experience as a zealot, but with an eye to the current situation in the Roman churches."[24] Furthermore, the speech is formulated in generic terms to ensure that a wide range of individuals would be capable of applying the argument to themselves, regardless of the extent to which they were aware of Paul's actual personal experiences. Jewett concludes that the character Paul constructs is Paul himself, albeit an earlier version thereof—namely, himself driven by zealous prejudice prior to his conversion.[25]

Will N. Timmins has attempted to swing the pendulum back again in the opposite direction by arguing that the *egō* is "a representative, paradigmatic 'I', but also one who is a believer in Christ who confesses an ongoing, Adamic, anthropological condition of fleshliness."[26] Of particular interest in the arguments that Timmins mounts against Stowers's interpretation is his

---

[21] Ibid., 763.

[22] Ruth Amossy, "Introduction to the Study of Doxa," *Poetics Today* 23 (2002): 369.

[23] Barthes, *S/Z*, 4.

[24] Jewett, *Romans*, 444.

[25] Ibid., 445. "Paul has decided to couch his argument concerning zealotism with *prosopopoeia* drawn from his own life, because it was rhetorically more effective than to mount a direct attack on similar problems in Rome itself. If Paul can convince his audience that zealous prejudice had been counterproductive for himself as a paradigmatic convert, he will be in a position to address the remnants of this legalistic tendency in the later sections of his letter."

[26] Will N. Timmins, *Romans 7 and Christian Identity: A Study of the 'I' in Its Literary Context* (Cambridge: Cambridge University Press, 2017), 8.

contention that the supposed change in voice in Romans 7 is indistinguishable from the writer's ("authorial") voice elsewhere in the letter: "There is too much of Paul's own Christian perspective in the characterisation."[27] In his review of the book, Elder critiques Timmins for not adequately dealing with the writer's address to an individual in Rom. 8:2. "The problem that this poses for his thesis is clear: if Paul is speaking in Rom 7:7–25, Paul then must be addressing himself as σε in Rom 8:2."[28] Timmins's approach throughout is to consider the "I" of Romans 7 in relation to Paul's anthropology generally, and therefore the "I" ultimately still serves as a character of a sort, albeit less that of an individual persona than of a more generic category that the writer himself also occupies. But the idea that the writer effectively addresses his own self has merit. The "I" of Romans 7 is not fictional because the Author-Paul steps momentarily outside of himself in order to perform and employ it. It is a fiction because the self of the implied author is already a fiction, and that fictional self is always fractured and split.

These interpretations[29] share in common the assumption that the "real" Paul, or some dimension or period thereof, is in some way or to some degree actually behind the work as an author, and either present in the work (i.e., Romans) or accessible through it if one exercises proper exegetical method and care. They depend upon and perpetuate the myth and symbol of "the Author," and with it an approach to the letter that views it as a work rather than a text. They view the author's voice made present in writing as a personal voice that guarantees or anchors the ideas expressed, and they regard the identity of the self as something best understood foremost in reference to history rather than to language or to writing. Nevertheless, the incorporation of aspects of characterization, performance, time, and perspective in the interpretations of Stowers, Seifrid, Lambrecht, Jewett, Elder, Timmins, and others provides a fruitful starting point—an exegetical rationale even—for pressing the implications and consequences of the writer's use of the first-person pronoun in

---

[27] Ibid., 25.

[28] Nicholas A. Elder, review of Will N. Timmins, *Romans 7 and Christian Identity: A Study of the 'I' in Its Literary Context*, *Review of Biblical Literature* [http://www.bookreviews.org] (2019), 4.

[29] Namely, the biographies of Paul produced largely on the basis of his explicit autobiographical statements in his letters and the indirect narrations of the self that are the letters, which are subsequently parsed and distilled in search of the remainder, the residue of the self; i.e., biographies wherein the self is an historical reality made up of the cumulative sum of so many identifiable and chronologically sequenced events, facts, etc., which then either are or are not represented in or by the work.

this passage. In fact, as I noted in the previous chapter, de Man contended that *prosopopoeia* was the fundamental characteristic of *all* autobiography, which is to say that it is the only thing that any autobiographical statement ever is: "The author reads himself in the text, but what he is seeing in this self-reflexive or specular moment is a figure or a face called into being by the substantive trope of prosopopoeia, literally, the giving of a face, or personification."[30]

Hence, what I think is overlooked in these debates is the possibility of identifying or locating the writing-self in or with something else, thinking of it more along the lines of something on the periphery, something that leaves a trace in the gaps and folds of both form and content but is never actually or fully present there. I am certain that no interpreter would presume that the entirety of Paul is to be found in the sum of his letters. But what I mean to say is that what we encounter here is not actually (i.e., really, literally, in substance, essentially) Paul in any manner, state, or moment.

If what we might refer to as the historical Paul is inaccessible through the self-narrative discourses he produces, who or what might be found instead? One of the questions driving this chapter concerns what relevance Barthes's experiment in "neutral" writing using autobiographical discourse might have for understanding differently the first-person pronoun in Rom. 7:14-25. How might we read the "I" in this passage alongside *Roland Barthes by Roland Barthes* (RB) so as to set aside (if not abandon altogether) questions of whether or to what extent it represents an historical figure, and if so, at which point in that author's life, while at the same time discovering something of both the writer and the work (i.e., of writing), at the moment of writing, in relation to the self, one's ideas, and matters of time and point of view inherent in narrative discourse? In this chapter, I aim to reread and rewrite the "I" of Rom. 7:14-25 in a manner that does not seek to identify and articulate any matters of fact with respect to the historical Paul who is understood to have authored this letter, but instead to focus on the "I" as a character-narrator speaking about a self in relation to both a past and a present, confronted with both the insurmountable power of writing and the utter fragility and inadequacy of language. In other words, the real Paul does not voice a specific fictional or conceptual character but the self-as-character. My suggestion is that the

---

[30] Anderson, *Autobiography*, 12.

"I" of Romans 7 is neither fully Paul's own self nor an altogether fictive other serving as a device of the author. It is a literary figuration of the writing-self in the moment of writing, a refraction of the self's plight in writing—that is, of the conscription, fabrication, and figuration of the subject in self-narration, encountered peripherally by the reader as in a rustle. The ruminations of the writer of Romans seem to resemble those of André Gide: "I am anxious to know what I shall be; I do not even know what I want to be; but I do know that I must choose. . . . I don't know what I ought to want. I am aware of a thousand possibilities in me, but I cannot resign myself to want to be only one of them. And every moment, at every word I write, at each gesture I make, I am terrified at the thought that this is one more ineradicable feature of my physiognomy becoming fixed."[31]

In *The Pleasure of the Text*, Barthes describes the tantalizing and desirous quality of that which occupies intermediate space: "In perversion . . . it is intermittence . . . which is erotic: that of the skin scintillating between two pieces (pants and sweater), between two edges (open shirt, glove, and sleeve); it is this very scintillation which seduces, or rather: the staging of an appearance-disappearance."[32] This, I would argue, is the manner in which the author (not as an authority but as a writer) appears in the text, according to Barthes: namely, through flickering glimpses of the insubstantive (in both senses of the term), insignificant, and impermanent.

Self as Character

Twice in *RB*, Barthes states provocatively, "All this must be considered as if spoken by a character in a novel—or rather by several characters."[33] This is an intriguing, and by now quite apt, perspective on both the self and self-narration,

---

[31] André Gide, *Journals Volume 1: 1889-1913*, trans. Justin O'Brien (Urbana: University of Illinois Press, 1947), 18.

[32] Barthes, *Pleasure*, 9–10. Cf., Gallop, *Deaths of the Author*, 150, n. 24.

[33] Barthes, *Roland Barthes*, 1 and 119. The phrase, "or rather by several characters," appears only in the second instance, and Barthes goes on to explain, "for the image-repertoire, fatal substance of the novel, and labyrinth of levels in which anyone who speaks about himself gets lost—the image-repertoire is taken over by several masks (*personae*), distributed according to the depth of the stage (and yet *no one—personne*, as we say in French—is behind them. . . . nothing is more a matter of the image-system, of the imaginary, than (self-) criticism. The substance of this book, ultimately, is therefore totally fictive" (119–20; emphasis in original).

and while I would consider it an appropriate framing of all autobiographical discourse, it seems to me an especially fitting description of the situation in Rom. 7:14-25. The statement highlights how the self can only ever be written as a figure emplotted in narrative, which is in turn complicated not least of all by the dynamics of focalization and time.[34]

RB is an example of Barthes's larger ongoing interest in both "neutral" writing and "the writer" (i.e., as opposed to an author). What Barthes termed "neutral" writing is writing that "resists the tendency in language to revert to the signified (stable meaning)," seeking instead "to undermine or simply absorb writing (language on the level of the signifier)."[35] As an experiment in this endeavor, *RB* engages in writing as an intransitive verb, that is, by attempting to sidestep writing *something* in favor of simply writing.[36] Hence, just before the second instance in which Barthes recommends reading the words of *RB* "as if spoken by a character in a novel," he states:

> His "ideas" have some relation to modernity, i.e., with what is called the avant-garde . . .; but he resists these ideas: his "self" or ego, a rational concretion, ceaselessly resists them. Though consisting apparently of a series of "ideas," this book is not the book of his ideas; it is the book of the Self, the book of my resistances to my own ideas; it is a *recessive* book (which falls back, but which may also gain perspective thereby).[37]

Barthes sought to disentangle the associated identity of one's "thought" or "ideas" from one's "self," especially when it was someone else pigeonholing him, projecting on him a particular identity based on what they perceived as the connotation of his thoughts, aiming to "decide" him, to fit him to a system by means of categorization. "The writer's freedom that Barthes describes is, in

---

[34] The first instance of Barthes's statement concerning how his autobiographical writing should be taken appears on what would be page 1, were it numbered, i.e., directly opposite the copyright page. It appears both in French as an image of Barthes's handwriting and in italicized English typeface. The forty-one pages that follow feature a collection of images, accompanied by captions, commentary, and glosses of various sorts. Barthes describes the images as "the author's treat to himself, for finishing his book. . . . I have kept only the images that enthrall me," he writes, "without my knowing why (such ignorance is the very nature of fascination, and what I shall say about each image will never be anything but . . . imaginary)" (3). The split between third-person ("the author . . . himself") and the first-person pronouns ("I . . . me") occurs throughout the book, highlighting the inescapable split between the writing-self and the self that it inscribes. These images and their inclusion reflects the tension that results from writing oneself as an Other.

[35] Graham Allen, *Roland Barthes* (London: Routledge, 2003), 95.

[36] Jonathan Culler, *Barthes: A Very Short Introduction* (Oxford: Oxford University Press, 1983), 87; see Roland Barthes, "To Write: An Intransitive Verb?," in *The Rustle of Language* (1966), 11–21.

[37] Barthes, *Roland Barthes*, 119; emphasis in original.

part, flight. The writer is the deputy of his own ego—of that self in perpetual flight before what is fixed by writing, as the mind is in perpetual flight from doctrine."[38] Consequently, speaker, writer, and self cannot be equated or used synonymously. Similarly, I see in Romans 7 the writer of the letter attempting to distance himself from his thoughts. What strikes me as curious is that scholarly conclusions regarding the letter and its writer seem intent on attempting to do likewise, but they do so from a different point of reference insofar as they separate what they identify as Paul's thought from that of an Other lest they contaminate.

Romans 7:25 would appear at first blush to reflect some sort of Cartesian division or distinction between mind and body: "With my mind I am a slave to the law of God, but with my flesh I am a slave to the law of sin." However, Barthes's resistance to his ideas in *Roland Barthes* is not premised on any such differentiation. Rather, it reflects Barthes's refusal of reduction, reification, and rigidity in favor of an unwavering insistence on plurality, materiality, and fluidity.[39]

In "Barthes to the Third Power," which is nothing other than Barthes's review of his own book, Barthes describes *RB* as having "been written solely to refuse meaning."[40] He describes the writer, "Barthes," as "playing the fool"[41] in order to "exorcise" the "Stupidity" with which he is obsessed,[42] and describes "the creation of which the book is the locus" as existing "neither in the statements nor even in the writing, but essentially in the clandestine act whereby Barthes 'imagines himself' an idea, puts himself in quotation marks and then removes them: a dislocation which obviously lends itself to every sort of misunderstanding."[43]

In Rom. 7:14-25, the writer seems also to imagine the self—not a specific self, per se, concretely named and located, but the self generally—as an idea, something ephemeral and elusive, never fully autonomous or manifest, but rather always appearing peripherally as a site of warring laws (7:23), to the

---

[38] Sontag, "Writing Itself," xxviii.
[39] For examples, which are especially apropos of the present discussion, not only of the consequences that follow such reduction and reification but also of the interests that such maneuvers tend to serve, see Barthes, "Garbo's Face" and "Einstein's Brain" in *Mythologies*, 73–75 and 100–2.
[40] Roland Barthes, "Barthes to the Third Power," in *On Signs*, ed. Marshall Blonsky (1975; Baltimore: Johns Hopkins University Press, 1985), 189–91.
[41] Cf. my discussion of 2 Corinthians in Chapter 4.
[42] Barthes, "Barthes to the Third Power," 189.
[43] Ibid., 190.

point that the conflict itself becomes a law (7:21). Hence, the writer, seeking to exorcise a certain "stupidity," writes the "I" as a subject at the intersection of legal discourses, and resists those discourses with a narrative.

In *RB*, Barthes describes "stupidity" as

> a hard and indivisible kernel, a *primitive*: no way of decomposing it *scientifically* . . . . What is it? A spectacle, an aesthetic fiction, perhaps a hallucination? Perhaps we want to put ourselves into the picture? It's lovely, it takes your breath away, it's strange; and about stupidity, I am entitled to say no more than this: *that it fascinates me*. Fascination is the *correct* feeling stupidity must inspire me with . . . it grips me (it is intractable, nothing prevails over it, it takes you in an endless hand-over-hand race).[44]

An example of this "indivisible kernel" of "stupidity" emerges in *Mourning Diary*, a work in which Barthes reflects on the death of his mother, on his process of grappling with that loss, and on mourning as such. In the entry of November 12 he writes, "[Stupid]: listening to Souzay sing: 'My heart is full of terrible sadness,' I burst into tears." Barthes affixes a footnote to the name Souzay that reads: "whom I used to make fun of," referring to his essay, "The Bourgeois Art of Song" in *Mythologies*.[45] The point is not that Barthes has changed his mind regarding the myth of Souzay. Rather, his point concerns the inexplicable manner by which "Barthes" is struck when listening to Souzay sing, eliciting an unexpected, unintended emotional response, that stems from neither the music itself, per se, nor any innate quality it possesses, nor any newfound positive appreciation Barthes has for the artist or his music, but from some relationship it bears, *in time*, to Barthes's mourning of his mother, and also the manner in which it manifests and reflects the distance between his self and his work. "Stupidity" appears to be a sort of manifestation of what Barthes describes as "the neutral." The "neutral" is a response to the dichotomy of Doxa and its contrary, paradox.[46] But Barthes refuses to label it a third term and instead portrays it as "the second term of a new paradigm, of which

---

[44] Ibid., 51; emphasis in original.

[45] Barthes, *Mythologies*, 190–93.

[46] In his essay, "From Work to Text" (in *The Rustle of Language*, 56–64 [1971]) Barthes assigns a "work" to the arena of Doxa and juxtaposes a "text" as para-doxical by virtue of the way in which it "tries to locate itself very specifically *behind* the limit of the *doxa*" (58). The Neutral is an effort to exceed even that limitation, lest it fall victim to the same tendency toward censorship that characterizes public opinion, mass production, and naturalized language.

violence (combat, victory, *theatre*, arrogance) is the primary term."[47] Barthes's neutral writing is, in part, an attempt to articulate (i.e., in the etymological sense of dividing into joints and uttering distinctly) that which occupies the space between signifier and signified.

This mode of "neutral writing" in which Barthes is engaged is one that does not express or convey (i.e., something that exists beforehand and lies behind it) but is for its own sake and that resists summarization, concretization, crystallization, and condensation. The assertiveness that inherently character-izes language produces, according to Barthes, a "double discourse, whose mode has overreached its aim, somehow."[48] The initial remedy is to add qualifications, but these are incapable of unsettling language, "as if anything that came out of language could make language tremble."[49]

I see in Romans 7, on the part of the writer, a similar longing (and frustration) to write neutrally, without violence, to compose without assertion, to exorcise "stupidity," as it were, all of which manifests in an analogous sort of stammering. Barthes uses "stammering" to describe the act of "annulation-by-addition": the quality of speech whereby "what has been said cannot be unsaid, *except by adding to it.*"[50] Furthermore, I see the eruption of a double—and doubling—discourse that shows the "I" to be fundamentally fragmented. The acting "I" is not the writer but the sin within—a law that exhibits or manifests as "a law at war in my members" vis-à-vis "a delight . . . in my inmost self." Interpreters are wont to name the figure in Romans 7; to identify the referent of the "I"; to fix and locate the speaker; to recognize the *author*; and to articulate precisely his relationship to the ideas and to so many other "I"s—or rather to various ideas conflated and fused with various "I"s—communicated in the work. But while the "I" of Romans 7—like all literary characters—resembles a person, it is a "fabricated creature,"[51] a simulacrum, and both the writer and the "I" in

---

[47] Barthes, *Roland Barthes*, 132–33; my emphasis; see also Allen, *Roland Barthes*, 96.

[48] Barthes, *Roland Barthes*, 48.

[49] Ibid., 48. Hence, in *Roland Barthes*, Barthes shows himself, as a writer, anxious about his writing.

[50] See Barthes, "The Rustle of Language," 76; emphasis in original.

[51] Bal, *Narratology*, 115: "Characters resemble people. Literature is written by, for, and about people. That remains a truism, so banal that we often tend to forget it, and so problematic that we as often repress it with the same ease. On the other hand, the people with whom literature is concerned are not real people. They are fabricated creatures made up from fantasy, imitation, memory: paper people, without flesh and blood. That no satisfying, coherent theory of character is available is probably precisely because of this human aspect. The character is not a human being, but it resembles one. It has no real psyche, personality, ideology, or competence to act, but it does possess characteristics which make psychological and ideological descriptions possible."

Romans 7 resist nomination, in terms of both naming and being named. As a character, the "I" of Romans 7 occupies a neutral space: an *atopia*—as opposed to utopia, which Barthes describes as "reactive, tactical, literary, (proceeding) from meaning and governing it"[52]—with regard to the dichotomies that structure the argument and that assign identity to the respective parties and positionalities in view, drawing boundaries around them, imbuing them with a sense of substance, of meaning. Flesh and spirit, evil and good, action and desire, we and I, past and present, death and life, all represent assertions, a theater of conflict, drawn from the writer's "image-repertoire."[53] As we saw earlier, the image-repertoire is an inescapable trap: one recognizes oneself as a subject only in relation to one's image-repertoire. But the images never present the self directly; they only instigate a certain relation. In place of "the old written code" (Rom. 7:6), we have here a letter, transient and ephemeral. And in that work we encounter that which is appropriate to it: a literary character, a narrative figure that does not exist apart from the narrative of which it is a part, and that "speaks" what and where the self cannot. The "I" of Romans 7 is neither an essence nor a representative (i.e., whether of Paul, or "Adam," or the reader in Rome, etc.) but instead a particular narrative configuration that exists in its relation to concepts. The figure appears here in a work of writing as a writer in relation to a text.[54]

Focalization

Everything presented to a reader in and through a narrative is focalized. Focalization refers to the ideological position from which the narrative and elements or aspects thereof are presented. Focalization differs from point of view in that the latter pertains solely to the one seeing and/or narrating while the former concerns a larger conceptual framing of the narrative and/

---

[52] Barthes, *Roland Barthes*, 49.

[53] William Touponce, "Literary Theory and the Notion of Difficulty," in *The Idea of Difficulty in Literature*, ed. Alan C. Purves (Albany: SUNY Press, 1991). The "image-repertoire is a Barthesean concept that Touponce explains as "a set of images functioning as a misunderstanding of the subject by itself" (67).

[54] It is akin to the speaker in Barthes's *Lover's Discourse*, wherein "the amorous subject, the 'I' of Barthes's text, is a character in his own novel; or rather, the 'I' . . . is a character in a novel (of unrequited love, of the frustration of the Imaginary coming up against the Real) who wishes to be a character in another novel (in which the Imaginary becomes the Real)." Allen, *Roland Barthes*, 111–12.

or of various elements therein. There are different types of focalization (e.g., zero focalization, internal focalization, and external focalization[55]) and different levels of focalization (e.g., simple, compound, and complex). Simple focalization is rare and limited to narrator-focalizers. Character-focalization— that is, when a narrative situation or event is rendered in a manner governed by a particular character's point of view and conceptual perspective—is, on the other hand, always an instance of compound-focalization: the focalizing character is embedded within the larger focalization governing the narrative as a whole. It is not always possible to distinguish clearly between narrator-focalizers and character-focalizers, and such indeterminacy is indicative of complex focalization.

Who or what, in the narrative of Romans 7, is focalized? And where is the focalizer located? To begin, the passage is an instance of compound (character-)focalization. The "I" focalizes the struggle between action ("I do. . .," v. 16) and inaction ("I do not do. . ., v. 19), and between sin (". . .what I do not want," vv. 16 and 17) and desire (". . .the good I want," v. 19). Patrick O'Neill argues that "character-focalization is in principle *always unreliable*, since it is made available to the reader only through the mediation of a prior focalization, namely that of the narrator, whose words constitute the only textual level to which we have unmediated access."[56] We might, therefore, look to the narrator in order to find a stable point of reference and to locate the narrative's origin. However, we recognize that the narrator is not necessarily

---

[55] On focalization, see e.g., Gérard Genette, *Narrative Discourse: An Essay in Method*, trans. Jane E. Lewin (Ithaca, NY: Cornell University Press, 1980), 185–210; idem., *Narrative Discourse Revisited*, trans. Jane E. Lewin (Ithaca, NY: Cornell University Press, 1988), 64–78; David Herman, *Story Logic: Problems and Possibilities of Narrative* (Lincoln: University of Nebraska Press, 2002), 301–9; Manfred Jahn, "Focalization," in *The Cambridge Companion to Narrative*, ed. David Herman (Cambridge: Cambridge University Press, 2007), 96–100; Shlomith Rimmon-Kenan, *Narrative Fiction: Contemporary Poetics*, 2nd ed. (London: Methuen, 2002), 72–86; and Bal, *Narratology*, 142–61. Zero focalization is the result of an omniscient, unrestricted narrating position wherein the events and characters of the story world are narrated from a vantage point that that allows seeing across time and space, as well as into the minds of characters. The variability of zero focalization prevents its location from being clearly identified. In case of external focalization, everything is narrated from a position entirely outside of the story. Therefore, they tend to be comprised mostly of dialogue, the outward behavior of characters, and other observable phenomena. Finally, internal focalization focalizes the story through a specific character within it, restricting information to what is perceptible only to that character. Theorists commonly divide internal focalization into three subcategories depending on whether everything is narrated through a single character (fixed), or various story items are seen or narrated by different characters (variable), or individual events are viewed through several perspectives (multiple focalization).

[56] Patrick O'Neill, *Fictions of Discourse: Reading Narrative Theory* (Toronto: University of Toronto Press, 1996), 104.

identical to the author; narrators, too, are focalized, namely by the implied author. In fact, everything in a narrative is "ultimately—or rather *primarily*—focalized by the implied author, through the interposed lens of the narrator(s), and possibly also through the further lens of one or more characters."[57] Hence, theoretically, narrators are also potentially unreliable focalizers.[58] In Rom. 7:14-25, the narrative of struggle, the "theatre of conflict," and the evaluation of the discourses at war (signified by the elements of the image-repertoire) are presented from the point of view of the "I." Self-narration is always, of necessity, anecdotal. But the origin of the narrative voice is indeterminate, and the reliability of the speaker (and therefore of the speaker's assessments of the objects being viewed) is unstable. In the face of such ambiguity, "it is the context of how we think we are *supposed* to behave that ultimately decides for us"[59] whose view is presented and how to regard it. Hence, the decisions concerning whether or to what extent to identify the "I" as Paul and the internal struggle as his stem less from anything dictated or expressed by the work than from previous interpretive commitments on the part of the reader. For my part, I elect to regard the ambiguity and instability of the "I", split and doubled in its roles as focalizer and focalized, as writer and character, as itself "a hard and indivisible kernel" indicative of the nature of the self in writing.

Temporality

The narrative aspect of time factors heavily into both the narrative of Romans 7 and interpretations of the "I" vis-à-vis Paul. Jane Gallop's book *The Deaths of the Author* presents a richly layered exploration of Barthes's classic essay, "The Death of the Author," in which she identifies not only an "abstract, polemical

[57] Ibid., 97; emphasis in original.
[58] Ibid., 97. One might argue that, since Romans is a letter, we are not dealing with conventional narrative material in Chapter 7, and thus, it follows, there is no narrator but only an author. But if we grant the arguments of Seifrid, Lambrecht, Stowers, Jewett, and Elder that the "I" *is* a character, then we have also a narrative, which, by definition, indicates a narrator. In that case, one might argue that the narrator and the author are identical. But even Seifrid, Lambrecht, Stowers, Jewett, and Elder distinguish between the "I" of Romans 7 and the author.
[59] Ibid., 104; emphasis in original. "We will choose whichever particular reading seems most warranted by our overall reading of the situation as a whole, by our perception, that is to say, of the overall *context* involved. That perceived context, in turn, will be established by our notions of overall interpretive *relevance*" (102; emphasis in original).

death" so often associated with the now commonplace poststructuralist slogan, but also "a moving, more bodily death of the mortal author."[60] She argues that Barthes's essay does not present the author's death as "a simple dismissal" but rather as something that "institutes a relation in which the reader desires the author."[61] In the second half of the book, Gallop shifts from considering the author's death from the reader's perspective to a consideration of the author's death from the writer's point of view. She focuses on the combination of "personal mourning with intellectual work" in the genre of the "memorial essay."[62] Such modes of writing, in her view, highlight "the fragility of writing, a fragility that has everything to do with writing's temporal aspect," which is entangled with what she describes as the "general theoretical dilemma of obsolescence."[63]

Although it is not one of the works Gallop considers, her reflections recall again Barthes's *Mourning Diary*, in which writing, work, and death intersect explicitly, and in a manner that I think furthers my interpretation of the "I" in Romans 7. In the entry from November 14, Barthes writes, "One comfort is to see (in letters I've received) that many readers had realized what she was, what we were, by her mode of presence in 'RB.' Hence I had succeeded in that, which becomes a present achievement."[64] In another entry Barthes writes:

It's not solitude I need, it's anonymity (the anonymity of work).

I transform "Work" in its analytic meaning (the Work of Mourning, the Dream-Work) into the real "Work"—of writing.)

---

[60] Gallop, *Deaths of the Author*, 4–5. On temporality vis-à-vis life-writing, see also Stephen D. Moore, *Gospel Jesuses and Other Nonhumans: Biblical Criticism Post-poststructuralism* (Atlanta: Society of Biblical Literature, 2017). Drawing on the ways in which ". . . the time-interrogating works of queer theory . . . [have] sought to show that seemingly unassailably commonsensical categories like past, present, and future, together with history, chronology, and periodicity, are no less culturally constructed [i.e., than sex, gender, race, and ethnicity], no less politically contingent, no less intimately informed by the (il)logics of power and desire" (85–86), Moore demonstrates how "The Lukan Jesus is . . . the homohistorical Jesus who embodies a flattening and folding of difference and otherness into sameness, who is the Jesus of Luke's present, festooned with the christological titles of that present: Christ, Lord, Son of God, Son of Man, Savior. That present Jesus is retrojected into the past as Luke narrates his unhistory, and that past Jesus's future titles becomes his present property. Luke's homohistorical and unhistorical Jesus is the present become past and the past become future present" (88–89).
[61] Ibid., 5.
[62] Ibid., 10.
[63] Ibid., 11. She explains, "while a writer can revise and update if she chooses, the printed word is the province not of the writer but of the author. The printed word, necessarily anachronistic, is where the writer confronts her status as a dead author" (13).
[64] Barthes, *Mourning Diary*, 49.

for:

> the "Work" by which (it is said) we emerge from the great crises (love, grief) cannot be liquidated hastily: for me, it is accomplished only in and by writing.[65]

These two excerpts highlight two interrelated concepts relevant to my reading of Romans 7, both of which have something to do with the aspect of time in relation to the self in autobiographical discourse. On one hand, they depict the indirect, peripheral emergence or manifestation in the work of something or someone real and present in the life of the author by means of the writing itself. On the other hand, they illustrate the sense of the real—and, in this case, the self specifically—vanishing (rather than being expressed) in and through writing. "Writing at its best," writes Barthes, "is merely mockery. Depression comes when, in the depths of despair, I cannot manage to save myself by my attachment to writing."[66]

Like Barthes's mother in *RB*, someone or something comes through in Romans 7. And like Barthes himself in *Mourning Diary*, the "I" of Romans 7 searches desperately for a sort of anonymity, a neutral space and state freed of associations with ideas of the image-repertoire and of the body, both of which combine and crystallize in time, in a history marked by a vanishing present.[67] The "I" of Romans 7 is speaking of a resultant present in relation to a past. Marked by vacillation, the "I" oscillates between competing threats of absorption into a static idea, be it an "old written code" or "death."

While I think the majority, if not all, of the self-narrative moments throughout the letters discussed in this book reflect moments of ghostly, if not ghastly, haunting,[68] it is probably most pronounced in Romans 7. Verse 24 especially stands out: "Wretched man that I am! Who will rescue me from this body of death?" I think evidence of the haunting is partly manifest in the scholarly recoil in the face of it. Whereas so many "ordinary" readers might identify immediately with the struggle depicted, professional interpreters are wont to distance themselves from it. The most glaring example, as noted earlier, is the so-called "New Perspective" on Paul. The intentions, findings,

---

[65] Ibid., 132.
[66] Ibid., 62.
[67] See Barthes, "The Discourse of History."
[68] See Moore, *Gospel Jesuses*, 92–96.

and outcomes of the New Perspective are admirable, to be sure, but in the end they succumb to the same ideological mythologizing impulse, seeking to "salvage" Paul, as it were, selectively reading certain of Paul's statements in order to create a particular narrative.

Anderson points to the body as a central and recurring figure in *Roland Barthes* and notes that it is one Barthes "frees from notions of the known, discrete, singularized body."[69] At one point, he writes:

> The *corpus:* what a splendid idea! Provided one was willing to read *the body* in the corpus: either because in the group of texts reserved for study (and which form the corpus) the pursuit is no longer of structure alone but of the figures of the utterance; or because one has a certain erotic relation with this group of texts (without which the corpus is merely a scientific *image-repertoire*).[70]

Anderson sees in Barthes's refrains concerning the body the creation of a disturbance that affects, displaces, and mobilizes meaning. "For Barthes, the most 'meaningful' discourse is discourse which does not allow itself to be 'caught,' but which 'rustles' with different meanings, with a *frisson* or excitation which moves language away from definitive forms, from signs 'grimly weighted' by signifieds."[71] The writer of Romans, 1 and 2 Corinthians, and Philippians is similarly drawn to the body, and the figure of the body shows up in his autobiographical narratives. It is not necessary to read the forceful (re)emergence of the body as a site of war and death in Rom. 7:23 and 24 as a negative thing, for it is the very thing that disrupts and dislodges the images that would threaten to destroy through the conformity and assimilation of signification.

The narrative fiction of struggle and frustration in Romans 7 bears a striking similarity to what Barthes describes when he writes, with a hint of regret:

> I have the illusion to suppose that by breaking up my discourse I cease to discourse in terms of the imaginary about myself, attenuating the risk of transcendence; but since the fragment . . . is *finally* a rhetorical genre and since rhetoric is that layer of language which best presents itself to interpretation, by supposing I disperse myself I merely return, quite docilely, to the bed of the imaginary.[72]

---

[69] Anderson, *Autobiography*, p. 69.
[70] Barthes, *Roland Barthes*, 161; emphasis in original.
[71] Anderson, *Autobiography*, 69, referencing *Roland Barthes*, 97–98; emphasis in original.
[72] Barthes, *Roland Barthes*, 95.

Barthes's acknowledgment of his inability to fully or permanently escape both discourse and the image-repertoire by fragmenting it resonates with the text of the writer's self in Romans. However, it is not that the story of conflict *expresses* an internal contest or narrates an agonistic history that precedes it, whether on the part of an author or of a character. The writing is the very performance of struggle. The fragmentation at once resists, refracts, and reinstates the discourse and image-repertoire of the self. Traces of the same, *mutatis mutandis*, also occur in 1 and 2 Corinthians and Philippians. But in the process, a rustling is heard.

The author's death—both figurative and actual, in this case—does initiate a desire for the author.[73] Gallop says of Lévinas, "I want to hold on to this idea of the 'miracle of the trace' which allows us to 'hear' Lévinas speaking, allows him to speak in the present, even after his death."[74] So, too, readers want to hear in Romans 7 some semblance of the real, and I am no different in that regard. But the author we know, the one we call "Paul," is ultimately an anonymous writer, an implied author, a product of writing. But in the "I" of Romans 7, between references to "my inmost self" (7:22) and "my members" (7:23), I sense a fleeting glimpse, a trace of the author, whom I cannot otherwise, in any way, know. I do not mean an Author, but the writer. The embodied, carnal writer is diffused in the language of the written work, into a body of work. Through writing, the self is negated, replaced by an "I" that rustles.

Returning to the metaphor of rustling with which I began this chapter, Barthes used this term to imagine a situation in which "language would be enlarged . . . denatured to the point of forming a vast auditory fabric in which the semantic apparatus would be made unreal."[75] Language would be foregrounded, not to the absolute abandonment or denial of meaning, but in order to redefine meaning as "the vanishing point of delectation." Hence,

> The rustle . . . would be that meaning which reveals an exemption of meaning or—the same thing—that non-meaning which produces in the distance a meaning henceforth liberated from all the aggressions of which the sign, formed in the "sad and fierce history of men," is the Pandora's box.[76]

---

73 Gallop, *Deaths of the Author*, 5.
74 Ibid., 22.
75 Barthes, "Rustle of Language," 77.
76 Ibid., 78.

In Romans 7, I encounter a character occupying a neutral space between competing trajectories of time, perspective, and discourse. Both unable and unwilling to conclude "once and for all," the writer is left exhausted, beside himself (7:24, "Wretched *man* that *I* am!"), and with no recourse but to exclamation and abandonment: "Who will deliver me from this body of death?" What I take away from Romans 7 is a synecdochical figuration of the writing-self in the moment and space of writing. The "I" is a cipher for the plight of the subject in self-narration. The sound of rustling I hear is the figure in writing, which is at once and equally both present and absent by virtue of writing, and the exemption of meaning attached to the sign—the signature—of the author.

3

The Myth of Paul

By and large, New Testament scholars read Paul's statements in 1 Cor. 9:19-23 as referring to Paul's missionary strategy, which entailed participation in concrete practices associated with various groups. In the course of explicating Paul's remarks, they try to imagine what Paul seemed to be doing through the eyes of his Corinthian readers, and then reassert what they regard Paul as saying in a manner that is designed to identify with him and to share in his defense, regularly appealing to other New Testament letters of Paul in the process. The culminating move, then, is to posit Paul as a non-repeatable example, that is, as someone (some "thing" even) always to be emulated but never replicated, pursued but never attained.

If one surveys the work of scholars who have taken this approach in one way or another, who have reconstructed and explained the writer in this vein, one discovers that the "Paul" that emerges and is molded by the hands of biblical interpreters functions as a "myth" in the Barthesian sense of the term. "Paul" is constructed as a sign that in turn becomes a signifier in a second-order semiological system of meaning. I think Barthes's posthumously published lecture course, *The Neutral*, suggests a better way of reading this text in which the writer anticipates his own reception and speaks of a future in past tense—namely, as an instance of neutral writing. The "twinklings" of the Neutral in this passage resist appropriation and mythologization. The meaning that most interpreters extract from this passage is one that comes only at the expense of something that would otherwise "outplay" the systems of conflict necessary for there to be any meaning in the first place. In short, I contend that the customary interpretation of the passage is forced to violate the writer's effort to baffle a dominant structure by ultimately subjecting the writer again to a system dependent upon dichotomy.

My desire for the Neutral here stems, in part, from a sense of dissatisfaction, disappointment, and frustration. I see in so many readings of Paul a certain degree or sort of violence, often in the guise of liberation. I write in order to resist the tidal force operative in the discourse of biblical interpretation to make the words of the Bible transparent, thereby reducing them to a mechanism of conveyance for the transfer of meaning. My point is not that the writer of 1 Cor. 9:19-23 *intended* the Neutral, *avant la lettre*. Rather, I find in the passage a glimmer of the Neutral, largely because my desire for the Neutral emerges when I read both the passage and the traditional interpretations of it, and because I have wondered, like a character in David Mitchell's *Cloud Atlas*, "which 'I' he was when he dreamed."[1]

Becoming All Things

The writer of 1 Corinthians claims in 9:22b that "to all I have become all [things]." The statement bookends a similar claim at the start of the paragraph (9:19a): "For though I am free from all I made myself a slave." Between these two statements the writer lists a series of four figures: "I became to the Jews as a Jew"; "to those under law as under law"; "to those without law as without law"; and "I became to the weak weak." Throughout, the writer's stated aim in such adaptation is "that I might win some," which is then framed more broadly by the writer's desire to share in the gospel's blessings (v. 23).

The passage raises a number of questions. To what (or when) is the writer referring? In what manner has "Paul" (the name by which the author identifies himself in 1:1) become "as" this or that? That is to say, how does one who is a Jew by birth become as a Jew? And how does one alternate, for example, between being under law and without law? What law is in view? What specific legal practices did the writer have in mind, especially given the parenthetical caveats where the writer imposes limits on how a statement should be understood? What objectives were served by such alternating, becoming this then that, and in what way (other than the generally stated aim of "winning" or "saving" some and sharing in the gospel's blessings, that is)?

---

[1] David Mitchell, *Cloud Atlas: A Novel* (New York: Random House, 2004), 324.

Put differently, how does the act of "becoming as" help to achieve the goal? Do specific groups lie behind the various categories the writer names? Why, for instance, would the writer refer to both "Jews" and "those under (the) law" if he had in mind the same group? Is he speaking from his own perspective or from that of other parties, either those whom he became like or outside observers (e.g., the Corinthians)? How do the writer's statements here relate to the larger argument he is making in chapters 8–10 concerning whether one should consume food that has been sacrificed to idols, to the general situation in Corinth, and to the precarious and strained relationship between the writer and the Corinthian congregants?

The consensus among commentators is that the underlying referent of this paragraph concerns Paul's missionary strategy, what J. Paul Sampley terms his "evangelistic practice."[2] Elsewhere he explains: "[Paul's] voluntary slavery to all *involves a fundamental and exemplary accommodation to people as and where he finds them*."[3] Henry Chadwick describes the passage as a "confession . . . concerning [Paul's] principles of evangelism,"[4] which amounts to an apologetic technique[5] that is aimed at minimizing the gap between himself and his audience,[6] and that entails the reappropriation of language. It reflects "a general principle which dominated Paul's missionary work, namely, the renunciation of certain liberties in order to gain the greatest number of converts," writes Jean Héring.[7] According to William Orr and James Walther, it is a matter of "strategic accommodation."[8] Similarly, Günther Bornkamm describes the paragraph as "Paul's classical formulation of the maxim which characterized his whole missionary approach,"[9] though he is careful to stress

[2] J. Paul Sampley, *Walking Between the Times: Paul's Moral Reasoning* (Minneapolis: Fortress Press, 1986), 61.
[3] J. Paul Sampley, "The First Letter to the Corinthians: Introduction, Commentary, and Reflections," in *The New Interpreter's Bible* vol. X, ed. Leander E. Keck (Nashville: Abingdon Press, 2002), 907; emphasis in original.
[4] Henry Chadwick, "'All Things to All Men' (I Cor. ix.22)," *NTS* 1 (1954–1955): 261.
[5] Ibid., 269.
[6] Ibid., 270.
[7] Jean Héring, *The First Epistle of Saint Paul to the Corinthians*, trans. A. W. Heathcote and P. J. Alcock (London: The Epworth Press, 1962), 81.
[8] William F. Orr and James Arthur Walther, *1 Corinthians* (Garden City, NY: Doubleday, 1976), 239. Cf. P. Richardson, "Pauline Inconsistency: I Corinthians 9:19-23 and Galatians 2:11-14," *NTS* 26 (1979/80): 347–62, who argues that such accommodation is the unique privilege of apostles, but the principle of self-denial it exemplifies pertains to everyone.
[9] Günther Bornkamm, "The Missionary Stance of Paul in 1 Corinthians 9 and in Acts," in *Studies in Luke-Acts: Essays Presented in Honor of Paul Schubert*, eds. L. E. Keck and J. L. Martyn (Nashville: Abingdon Press, 1966), 194.

"how little the passage has to do with a mere art of adjustment or a successful missionary technique."[10]

Most scholars argue that Paul is responding to accusations of inconsistency and instability by defending his practice of accommodation. Although Chadwick suggests that it was Paul's teaching that underwent adjustment in relation to respective audiences,[11] most argue that it had to do with matters of custom, communal practices, what some refer to as *adiaphora* ("indifferent things"). For Hans Conzelmann, "Jewish customs" are in view.[12] Craig Keener labels them "cultural accommodations."[13] Gordon Fee identifies the referent as social (i.e., group) associations.[14] Bornkamm describes Paul's "maxim" as indicating "a practical stance of solidarity with various groups,"[15] and suggests that Paul is urging each individual member of such groups "to renounce for the sake of the other the use of his own [authority]."[16] Orr and Walther refer to Paul's statement and stance as "a breathtaking relativizing of national and legal values to the absolute value of the gospel."[17] Nina Nikki resolves the tension by appealing to "social identity" as distinct from "personal identity."[18]

Whatever the specifics,[19] exegetes imagine the readers in Corinth questioning, in light of Paul's behavior, pronouncements, and advice, whether or to what extent Paul held fast to any fundamental belief, doctrine, or theology, and wondering whether he was in fact guided by the spirit or if his actions were determined more forcefully by "the flesh" and the situations in which he found himself (cf. 2 Cor. 1:13-24). From the Corinthians' point of view, the situation reflected in Paul's words was an "apparently chameleonlike stance in matters of social relationships,"[20] one that struck them as "opportunistic"[21]

---

[10] Ibid., 197.

[11] Chadwick, "All Things to All Men,'" 261 and 263.

[12] Hans Conzelmann, *1 Corinthians* (Philadelphia: Fortress Press, 1975), 160.

[13] Craig S. Keener, *1–2 Corinthians* (Cambridge: Cambridge University Press, 2005), 81.

[14] Gordon D. Fee, *The First Epistle to the Corinthians* (Grand Rapids: Eerdmans, 1987), 423.

[15] Bornkamm, "Missionary Stance," 202.

[16] Ibid., 203.

[17] Orr and Walther, *1 Corinthians*, 243.

[18] Nina Nikki, "The Flexible Apostle: Paul's Varied Social Identifications in 1 Corinthians 9 and Philippians 3," in *Others and the Construction of Early Christian Identities*, 75–101, eds. Raimo Hakola, Nina Nikki, and Ulla Tervahauta (Helsinki: Finnish Exegetical Society, 2013), 77–88.

[19] I will return to this matter below. There are two things to note: (i) the specificity being ascribed by interpreters where there is none by Paul, and (ii) the "rustling" on the part of the writer, which results from the shuttling from one thing to another. This alternation, even by scholarly accounts, is the thing foremost in view, but it is also the thing they ultimately halt and fix.

[20] Fee, *Corinthians*, 423.

[21] Conzelmann, *1 Corinthians*, 159.

and "utilitarian,"[22] perhaps even ambiguous, conformist, and marked by "unprincipled vacillation,"[23] an "elasticity of principle."[24] And Paul's argument manifests a "phenomenon of oscillation."[25] Paul, it seems, was acting in a way that some may regard as consistent with an "ordinary turncoat who adjusts his habits for the sake of his own gain."[26]

In relation to the larger argument unfolding in the letter and the circumstances that occasioned it, the consensus is that Paul is arguing for his freedom *to* act thus. Scholars contend that he is defending his right to move freely and to conduct himself in accordance with the norms of various groups precisely because he was Christ's slave and belonged to no one else. Keener suggests that "Paul may be hinting at some dissatisfaction with his refusal to accept support."[27] He refuses to be beholden to those who would act as patrons to him, obliged to the requisite debts and honors associated with occupying the role of their client. Paul's "payment" is the conversion and salvation of others, and his own participation in the blessings of the gospel.

While the specific question of financial support may well be in play, it is only an instance, a case in point. More generally, an alternative mode of being in the world is what drives the claims Paul is making. Fredrik Grosheide explains: "Paul does have a certain liberty but he does not use it fully for that would be abusing it and it would hurt the progress of the gospel."[28] The exercise of his freedom, according to Orr and Walther, "did not take the form of flaunting his independence, however, by obstreperous nonconformity; but it took the opposite form of changing his conformity according to the people with whom he was dealing."[29]

In order to answer the questions posed above and to make sense of the passage, commentators regularly turn to statements in other letters of Paul. Chadwick, for example, appeals to Colossians. Bornkamm draws on Luke's portrayal of Paul in Acts and, although he considers Acts largely unreliable and irrelevant for the purposes of understanding 1 Cor. 9:19-23, he identifies

22 Ibid., 161.
23 Bornkamm, "Missionary Stance," 197.
24 Chadwick, "'All Things to All Men,'" 262.
25 Ibid., 265.
26 Orr and Walther, *1 Corinthians*, 243.
27 Keener, *1–2 Corinthians*, 77; cf. Bornkamm, "Missionary Stance," 194; F. W. Grosheide, *Commentary on the First Epistle to the Corinthians* (Grand Rapids: Eerdmans, 1953), 211.
28 Grosheide, *First Epistle to the Corinthians*, 211.
29 Orr and Walther, *1 Corinthians*, 243.

Acts 21:17-26 as "one historical example of what Paul meant."[30] Richardson treats 1 Cor. 9:19-23 in relation to Gal. 2:11-14 in order to resolve the apparent contradiction between the two passages, and he does so with reference to 2 Corinthians, Romans, and even Colossians. Grosheide makes reference to Acts, 2 Corinthians, 2 Thessalonians, Romans, and Philippians.

Having determined what it is that Paul is referring to (viz., his strategy for propagating the gospel) and the guise of Paul's "becoming as," interpreters customarily adopt an apologetic position, wherein they defend him against the implicit charges of being wishy-washy and duplicitous, asserting that underlying Paul's actions is a fundamental integrity. Grosheide finds in this section of 1 Corinthians "a deep insight . . . into the soul of the apostle." He identifies in 9:19-23 an important distinction between Paul's "objective condition" as one free from everyone and his "subjective condition" as one who has enslaved himself voluntarily to others.[31] This essential integratedness at the core of Paul's self and identity assures us that the "real" Paul is not what he appears, that is, he is not what his actions of "becoming as" one thing and then another might suggest. Any conclusion to the contrary reflects a problem of misunderstanding on the part of the audience, reader, etc., not Paul himself.

Finally, commentators take up the question of whether or to what extent Paul is to be imitated, whether his way of doing things is posited as a model for others to follow. Fee, wondering how it is that one can alternate between being under law and without law, states the answer most forcefully: "The paragraph does *not* offer a model of *self-restraint*, but of something considerably different—abstinence or indulgence . . . depending on the context."[32] He later explains that "Paul is not here speaking in generalities about his *modus operandi*; rather, he is defending past actions."[33] Sampley, on the other hand, states: "Paul, the exemplary strong, the free person, stands in an imitable way with the weak in the gospel, on account of the gospel, as a requirement of the gospel. As he does, so should every believer."[34]

I find these "solutions" (assuming there is any "problem" in the first place) unsatisfying. While they appear to explain, more or less, certain mechanical

---

[30] Bornkamm, "Missionary Stance," 205.
[31] Grosheide, *First Epistle to the Corinthians*, 211.
[32] Fee, *Corinthians*, 424, n. 10; emphasis in original.
[33] Ibid., 426, n. 21.
[34] Sampley, "First Letter to the Corinthians," 908.

aspects of Paul's rhetoric, certain surface-level functions of his argument, the riddle they aim to solve is one of the interpreters' own making. In smoothing out the rough edges that pose obstacles to, and even resist, meaning, they rob the writer's language of something more productive, despite appearing to appreciate the subtlety and complexity of what the writer says. Furthermore, they ultimately perform something other than what they claim. In the guise of explicating Paul's words, they first manufacture a particular notion or conceptualization of Paul, and then employ what they have constructed both to undergird the construction and to leverage it for the furtherance of larger ideologies related to the Bible and its interpretation. In other words, whereas these interpretations purport to provide us with access to the subject, "Paul," they in fact contribute to the mythologization of Paul by doing three things. They resist a natural identification with the Corinthians that would see the writer as waffling and insist instead on Paul's consistency. They appeal to a body of work as the expression of an author in the absence of the author himself. And they present "Paul," paradoxically, as an inimitable example to be imitated. In other words, there is a curious and yet eminently necessary and productive irony at the heart of their interpretations: readers can imitate the manifestations of Paul (e.g., they can become weak, *like* him), but they cannot imitate the essentially strong Paul. The figure of this "Paul" becomes at once both the product and the foundation of persistent ideologies of the self, language-as-communication, writing-as-expression, and of the very notion of imitation. In short, "Paul," in the hands of interpreters, functions as a myth in service to greater ends.

The Mythology of Paul

Roland Barthes uses the term "myth" to designate "phony instances of the obvious."[35] For Barthes, "myth" is not a matter of topic, story, or veracity, but rather a particular "type of speech . . . a mode of signification, a form."[36] The sort of myth that concerns Barthes has little to do with content (i.e., "the

---

[35] Barthes, *Mythologies*, xi. Barthes describes the collection as a semiological analysis of fifty-three "figures of rhetoric" or "mythologies" highlighting the confusion of "Nature" and "History," and his project as an effort "to expose in the decorative display of what-goes-without-saying the ideological abuse" that he sees hidden therein.

[36] Ibid., 217.

object of its message"). Since "it is human history which converts reality into speech,"[37] or which transforms closed, silent material into something "open to appropriation by society,"[38] he regards myth as the imposition of ideology in disguise: "ideas-in-form."[39]

> This is the point: we are no longer dealing here with a theoretical mode of representation: we are dealing with *this* particular image, which is given for *this* particular signification. Mythical speech is made of a material which has *already* been worked on so as to make it suitable for communication: it is because all the materials of myth . . . presuppose a signifying consciousness, that one can reason about them while discounting their substance.[40]

Barthes uses two instances of mythological speech in his essay, "Myth Today," in order to unpack and explain the operation of mythologization: a sentence from Latin grammar, and an image from the cover of a *Paris-Match* magazine. In the first instance, one encounters the phrase: "*quia ego nominor leo.*" While the words have, in and of themselves, a simple meaning ("because my name is lion"), they appear in the grammar in order to signify something else entirely: namely, "I am a grammatical example." The latter signification is in fact—and by force—the greater signification, the primary signification, the "idea" or "meaning" that matters most for the purposes of the one writing the grammar. Barthes identifies it as "a particular, greater semiological system, since it is coextensive with the language."[41] In the second instance, "a young Negro in French uniform is saluting, with his eyes uplifted, probably fixed on a fold of the tricolor."[42] While this is itself the meaning of the photograph—what it says, what is signified is "that France is a great Empire, that all her sons, without any color discrimination, faithfully serve under her flag, and that there is no better answer to the detractors of an alleged colonialism than the zeal shown by this Negro in serving his so-called oppressors."[43] The function of these "statements" is not to express but to illustrate. Moreover, it is to illustrate something altogether other than the "language" of the statement or image itself.

---

[37] Ibid., 218.
[38] Ibid.
[39] Ibid., 221.
[40] Ibid., 218–19.
[41] Ibid., 225.
[42] Ibid.
[43] Ibid.

It is my contention that the "Paul" at the heart of so many scholarly interpretations of 1 Corinthians (and of any other letter ascribed to Paul and deemed "authentic," for that matter) is a myth, not unlike so many other "figures of rhetoric" in Barthes's collection. For example, one of the figures Barthes analyzes in *Mythologies* is "Plastic."[44] He describes the process of its production as "the magical operation par excellence: the conversion of substance."[45] Between the raw materials and "the perfect human object" lies "nothing but a trajectory."[46] Hence, "more than a substance, plastic is the very idea of its infinite transformation . . . it is ubiquity made visible; moreover, this is the reason why it is a miraculous substance: a miracle is always a sudden conversion of nature."[47] In other words, plastic "is less an object than the trace of movement."[48] Plastic exerts a forceful ideological effect that transcends both the productiveness and productions of the material itself. Barthes identifies it as a "perpetual astonishment, the reverie of man at the sight of the proliferations of substance, detecting the connections between the singular of its origin and the plural of its effects."[49] This astonishment engenders pleasure because "it is by the scope of transformations that man measures his power."[50]

According to Barthes, "the price to be paid for this success is that plastic, sublimated as a movement, almost fails to exist as a substance."[51] Plastic is fundamentally "a *shaped* substance."[52] He argues that "the fashion for plastic highlights an evolution in the myth of the simili."[53] Plastic is not so much about actual production as it is about *imitation*. And here is the rub: "For the first time, artifice aims for the common, not for the rare. And thereby nature's ancestral function has been modified: it is no longer the Idea, the pure Substance which is to be regained or imitated; an artificial substance, more fecund than all the world's deposits, will replace it, will command the very invention of shapes."[54] Barthes's essay on plastic strikes me as a fruitful intertext

---

[44] Ibid., 193–95.
[45] Ibid., 193.
[46] Ibid.
[47] Ibid.
[48] Ibid.
[49] Ibid., 194.
[50] Ibid.
[51] Ibid.
[52] Ibid., 194; emphasis in original.
[53] Ibid., 194.
[54] Ibid., 195.

and analog for thinking about what is happening in traditional interpretations of 1 Cor. 9:19-23.[55]

I see a number of points of contact between the "Paul" that surfaces in the work of commentators and the figure of plastic as read by Barthes. To begin, plastic is itself something made, a product. It is a composite, fabricated substance, unnatural. It is then, in turn, something with which to make other things, an ingredient, a material. Similarly, "Paul" is a composite, a construction, which is then in turn the means by which so many other things are constructed and produced, whether it is histories of early Christianity or contemporary disciples. This process of production is most pronounced in the way interpreters regularly make sense of the writer's statements by consulting other letters bearing the same authorial name. While consulting and appealing to statements made in other letters said to have been written by Paul is pretty standard procedure in biblical studies, I make note of it primarily because this appeal to a body of work seems to violate one of the most fundamental requirements of historical-critical methodology: namely, contextual reading, understanding, and interpretation. In an effort to access, understand, and explicate the body of an historical subject, they appeal to a body of literary work. The assembly of an apparently stable persona requires a corpus in order to overcome the divided "I" reflected in the passage itself (viz., in v. 20, "though I myself am not under the law," and v. 21, "though I am not free from God's law"), which is a metonymy for a fundamentally fragmented self that is reflected in a collection of letters. But the collection of Paul's *oeuvre* contained within the New Testament and the canonical "context" it produces come after the letter of 1 Corinthians itself. They were not available to the Corinthian readers. Modern interpreters cannot help but argue alongside and in support of "Paul" in his defense because the canon functions as a "semiotic mechanism" shaping the reading process.

George Aichele points out in *The Control of Biblical Meaning* that the question of the canon is one that concerns the source and location of meaning: "a canonical text 'survives' as a meaningful book, not because of something

---

For the purposes of this chapter, I am focusing only on Barthes's analysis of plastic as a myth vis-à-vis the mythologization of Paul by interpreters. However, plasticity is also analogous to the dynamic of malleability reflected in what the writer says in 1 Cor. 9:19-23.

that is 'in' the text itself, but because of the exercise of institutional power."[56] The concept of canon reflects a desire on the part of a community for "a text that conveys truly an essential, authoritative message and that controls the interpretation of the message."[57] Ultimately, a canon reflects "a desire for identity, for power, and for meaning."[58] Just as Aichele regards "history itself as a semiotic construct, a story produced in the present,"[59] I am suggesting that the figure of "Paul," by virtue of its mythologization, is not an historical subject but a semiotic construct, a character in a narrative written by interpreters. We shift from Paul's *work* and Paul-as-*work* to Paul-as-*text*.

Furthermore, Paul, the person, becomes indistinguishable from "Paul," the idea. Like plastic, the subject is completely engulfed in the usage to which he is put.[60] "Paul" does not even exist apart from the narratives in which he is encased and the ideologies he is made to serve. "Paul," constructed by these readings of words (taken by interpreters to be expressive of an author) is more "fecund" than would be the historical subject. The "Paul" produced in these interpretations is more capable of producing offspring, more fruitful. The idea of "Paul" is fertile, marked by intellectual productivity, not on the part of an historical subject, but on the part of the interpretive machine that perpetuates his existence and the force it allows. Paul, long dead, remains ever-prolific. Having "become all things," Paul refracts something akin to what Barthes refers to as "plastic, sublimated as movement," and he, too, "almost fails to exist as a substance," or rather as a subject. The composite, plastic/plasticized Paul, is "an artificial substance," and his newly possessed fecundity will enable the invention of the inimitable that others should, nevertheless, always and forever strive to imitate.

In 1 Cor. 9:19-23, "Paul" embodies and perpetuates the aura of plastic, of plasticity, as it is captured in Barthes's essay. The effort on the part of commentators to pinpoint a stable, historical Paul behind the letters, that is, one who in fact is in some manner consistent, in order to ground the perceived

---

[56] George Aichele, *The Control of Biblical Meaning: Canon as Semiotic Mechanism* (Harrisburg, PA: Trinity Press International, 2001), 9.

[57] Ibid., 2.

[58] Ibid., 2; cf. Jonathan Z. Smith, "Sacred Persistence: Toward a Redescription of Canon," in idem., *Imagining Religion: From Babylon to* Jonestown (Chicago: University of Chicago Press, 1982), 36–52; Aichele, *Simulating Jesus*, 3–23.

[59] Aichele, *Control*, 8.

[60] See Barthes, *Mythologies*, 194.

accommodationist missionary strategy, necessitates, leads to, ultimately functions as, and perpetuates "an artificial substance," which is indeed "more fecund" than any raw materials that precede it. Fee concludes: "Paul's actions, which appear to them to be inconsistent, have integrity at a much higher level."[61] One cannot help but feel that "integrity" here carries a double notion: "Paul" is not only undivided but also morally upright. That, arguably, is the greater concern, too, because Paul functions as an authority, a standard of judgment, and an example.

It might seem that a "more fecund" Paul would suit the writer's subsequent invitation to "imitate" him in 1 Cor. 11:1. But what precisely is imitated, and in what manner? Elizabeth Castelli long ago argued persuasively that the language of imitation in Paul's letters functions as a strategy of power. "It articulates and rationalizes as true and natural a particular set of power relations within the social formation of early Christian communities."[62] Mimesis in Paul's context always involves a hierarchical relationship of derivation on the part of the copy vis-à-vis the model. Furthermore, it privileges sameness (especially in terms of unity and harmony) over difference (associated with "diffusion, disorder, and chaos"). And, finally, it is undergirded by a notion of authority.[63] The issue is one of operation rather than meaning: "Mimesis must be understood . . . as a notion that places sameness at a premium and imbues the model with a privileged and unattainable status."[64] What interests me here is the manner in which this same discourse of power is operating at the level of interpreters who posit the Paul of 1 Cor. 9.19-23 as an ideal example that is irreplicable, non-repeatable, and unachievable: an inimitable object of imitation.

The aspect of the mythologization of Paul that most contributes to its function as a myth is its indirect presentation. Recalling the comment from Sampley above concerning "Paul, the *exemplary* strong" who "stands in an imitable way with the weak" as "every believer" should, what is at issue is the very notion of example itself. For commentators like Sampley, Paul exemplifies accommodation in matters of no consequence (i.e., vis-à-vis

---

[61] Fee, *Corinthians*, 431.
[62] Elizabeth A. Castelli, *Imitating Paul: A Discourse of Power* (Louisville: Westminster John Knox, 1991), 15.
[63] Ibid., 16.
[64] Ibid., 89.

salvation). Paul's tendency is one of adaptation in matters deemed to be in some way secondary to, and distinct from, both the self and "the gospel." They are matters of culture, or of ethnic distinction, or of religious custom, as if such things are always only linked to "what really matters" (the self, the gospel) by the conjunction "and" rather than symbiotically (and semiotically) conditioning and conditioned by "the self" and "the gospel." Admittedly, much of what Paul writes seems to lend itself perfectly well to this sense. However, what is at issue is the shift whereby "the associative total of a concept and image ['Paul' in this case] in the first system becomes a mere signifier in the second,"[65] thus functioning as a myth that communicates a meaning much weightier and ultimately more *significant* than was previously possible when the resulting signifier was itself a sign. It is adaptability itself, not Paul, that is exemplified. It is not Paul the man we are to imitate, but Paul the infinitely variable and infinitely applicable, the persistent and perpetual, *idea*. Because he is both inaccessible and singular, Paul the man is inimitable. Hence, the "Paul" in view when exegetes explicate this text is the one that exemplifies example itself.

I do not think interpreters *intend* to mythologize Paul, but that is why it is a problem. It is an inescapable consequence of their effort to clarify and explicate the passage, particularly in a way consistent with the idea of "Paul" that authorizes and is authorized by the letter. Interpreters are forced to impose a meaning on the text, which supplements and ultimately supplants the text itself. But what suffers most in this mythologization of Paul is the very thing that captures the attention of readers in the first place. Although interpretations would appear to posit an appreciation for the sophistication of Paul's rhetoric and ideas, Paul's mode is ultimately oversimplified, the rustling is silenced and quashed, and Paul himself is reified.

There is an alternative to this approach, and there is something to be gained by entertaining it. The alternative refuses either to concretize or to crystallize aspects of the text that resist meaning. It refuses to fix the fluidity. And it offers an opportunity for a reading that does not require violence and imposition, one that leaves open the possibility of a different experience of the text. The alternative stems from what Barthes terms "the Neutral."

---

[65] Barthes, *Mythologies*, 223.

A Twinkling of the Neutral

Instead of evidence that undergirds the mythology of Paul that I have just described, I identify in 1 Cor. 9:19-23 "twinklings" of what Barthes labels "the Neutral." These fragments of the Neutral resist appropriation and mythologization. The Neutral results from Barthes's search for a third term that exceeds, transcends, and circumvents the oppositions that would otherwise allow for the imposition of meaning. Barthes describes "the Neutral as that which outplays the paradigm, or rather I call Neutral everything that baffles the paradigm."[66] The paradigm of which he speaks is "the opposition of two virtual terms from which, in speaking, I actualize one to produce meaning."[67] It is "the wellspring of meaning [because] meaning rests on conflict (the choice of one term against another), and all conflict is generative of meaning: to choose *one* and refuse the *other* is always a sacrifice made to meaning, to produce meaning, to offer it to be consumed."[68] The Neutral (i.e., *le neuter*, which could also be rendered "the Neuter") is that which does not fit the binary paradigm. Barthes's lecture course is structured around a collection of what he terms "twinklings." These are fragments not *of* the Neutral, per se, but rather "in which, more vaguely, there is some Neutral."[69] The figures[70] Barthes presents in his discussion of the Neutral are not offered as demonstrations. Rather, "each figure is at the same time search for the Neutral and performance of the Neutral."[71]

I see in 1 Cor. 9.19-23 three twinklings or refractions of the Neutral: (i) in the writer's use of "as" when describing his "having become" in reference to "Jews," "those under law," and "those without law," and also the absence of the word when he refers to "the weak"; (ii) at vv. 20 and 21 when the writer interjects caveats: "though not being myself" and "not [myself] being"; and (iii) in the word "weak" itself. In each instance, there is a kind of rustling, and the writer resists, or at least the passage poses an obstacle to, mythologization.

---

[66] Barthes, *The Neutral*, 6.
[67] Ibid., 7.
[68] Ibid.
[69] Ibid., 10.
[70] Throughout this chapter, I have been using "figure" in a more or less rhetorical sense, and with respect to "Paul" in the sense of personality or character. Here, with reference to "the Neutral," the notion of figure shifts to Barthes's use of the term in *Lover's Discourse*, 3–4. Similarly, in *The Neutral*, commenting on the organizing principle and arrangement of the course and his selection of figures and fragments, Barthes states: "Figure; rhetorical allusion (= a circled piece of discourse, identifiable since titleable) + face that has an 'air,' an 'expression. . .'" (10).
[71] Barthes, *The Neutral*, 11, *sic*.

As

One of the more identifiable and attractive aspects or characteristics of the Neutral is its peripherality and fleetingness. The Neutral is ephemeral. This is partly what marks it as a fantasy, as *atopian*.[72] The drift of the Neutral can be seen in the writer's use of "as." The word *as* is tremendously ambiguous and slippery. It is a term associated with simile. Whereas metaphors assert a substantive sameness between two things, similes merely suggest. They do not speak directly or claim a precise identification. They hint at likeness and resemblance without disguising the inherent limitations of the juxtaposition. They are the stuff of simulation[73] and approximation.

As lacks precision. It offers far too little purchase upon which to build such a stately edifice as the one erected in the mythologized figure of "Paul." Yet, paradoxically, it is that ambiguity that also allows scholars to manufacture such a towering ziggurat. While this imprecision is precisely what compels exegetes to explain the writer's statements in the first place, it is then quickly overlooked and forgotten once interpreters feel they have pinpointed the referents and the manner of the writer's adaptation. When critics attempt to identify concretely who or what the various designations represent, or to get a fix on specific practices that would entail "becoming as" in the mind of the writer or his audience, or to home in on the mode of the writer's simulation, the simile breaks under the strain. Both the delightfulness of the language and any potentiality it might possess or allow for are muted and repressed. *As* is left to function only as an indication that the underlying integrity, the essence of Paul, remains intact, and to provide an assurance that any similarity between Paul and whatever he appears to be is only superficial.

The Neutral that glimmers in the words of this passage works against such flat conclusions, however. The writer's repeated refrain, "I became as," suggests something different and more nuanced than simply "I became." To be sure, interpreters are quick to note that the "obvious" reading is problematic. For example, Paul, a Jew, cannot again become a Jew. Nor can he be at once law-abiding and lawless. But I am suggesting that it is more than simply "problematic," because the issue is that it implies something fixed. The act of

---

[72] See Barthes, *Roland Barthes*, 49 and 76–77.

[73] Cf. Aichele's analysis of "reality effects" and the "simulations" or "simulacrums" of Jesus in the New Testament gospels (*Simulating Jesus*, especially 30–37).

Paul becoming "like" a Jew when he already is a Jew should make the reader pause in bewilderment, a bewilderment that defies explanation. The various terms of the equation (viz., "Jew," "under the law," "outside the law") are strained and forced to do double duty. Thus, the passage invites us to linger with *becoming*, which suggests process and fluidity, because *becoming as* places the emphasis not on the thing become but on the gesture and the rustling it affects.

As is the language of not quite, of almost. It embodies an inclination toward a third term that transcends the either/or paradigm of meaning and thereby upends the dichotomy. Thus, I see in the writer's use of *as* a mark or trace of the Neutral. It refracts a search for a third term, and an attempt to speak indirectly, nonviolently, without asserting. In the final statement of becoming, the writer breaks with the form of the previous three. He abandons *as* and states simply that he "became weak." Orr and Walther posit that "the absence of *hōs* is probably deliberate. This move on Paul's part is of a different sort than those in the preceding verses."[74] Unfortunately, they offer no further elaboration. My suggestion is that the sliding of simile at work in *as* will be made fully manifest in *weak*.

Not Being Myself

In 1 Cor. 9:20 and 21, the writer interrupts his assertion, attempts, in a manner of speaking, to qualify, overturn, stop short, to catch what he has just said before it runs away: "*not being myself* under the law," and "*though I am not* free from God's law." The effort to clarify results in a split, a fragmentation. But I regard this neither as a division in the sense of either/or nor as a doubling in the sense of both/and, nor as an essence versus a manifestation. Admittedly, the former holds some attraction if taken as a metonymy for the distinction between author and writer, for example, but the latter is particularly problematic insofar as it is precisely the mythology of "Paul" promoted by biblical interpreters when they argue for an underlying integrity in Paul behind his well-intentioned (i.e., conditioned and motivated by the gospel), but ultimately superficial (i.e., never indicative of the "real" Paul), adaptations. Hence, I read these interruptions

---

[74] Orr and Walther, *1 Corinthians*, 240.

instead as twinklings of the Neutral, an effort on the part of the writer to avoid the violence of meaning, of naming, of definition.

One reason for doing so is that the writer himself, it seems, tries to sidestep the simplicity of proffering examples. Despite the fact that commentators tend to lump together and gloss the various figures mentioned in 1 Cor. 9:19-23, the writer does not refer simply to "Jews" and "Gentiles," for example, but to "Jews," "those under law," "those without law," and "the weak." I detect a rather pointed randomness to this list of figures, a degree of arbitrariness. Like the poet, Christopher Poindexter, the writer of 1 Corinthians seems to identify or locate his self in relation to his context, and then at once to assign purpose to the incidental even as he retracts any permanence or solidity to the transient self so positioned. Poindexter writes:

> I used to tell myself
> "I drink to understand those I do not know.
> to feel what they feel. what he feels. what she feels."
> It is similar to my favorite bible verse but played with
> a little "to the drunkard I become the drunkard. To
> the stoner I become the stoner. To the weeping man I
> become the weeping man."[75]

Neither Poindexter's nor "Paul's" list functions comprehensively, much less exhaustively. In fact, had the writer of 1 Corinthians referred simply to "Jews" and "Gentiles," he may have been speaking more comprehensively, in certain respects, and "all" is already exhaustive, but its lack of specificity leaves too much to chance. The substantive use of the Greek word *pas* requires that one supply the word "things," and indeed Paul does become all *things* in the exegetical readings discussed above wherein the myth of "Paul" is overlaid and Paul's relational dynamic is transfigured, erased, supplemented, and replaced by the concrete that is necessary for meaning. Interpreters exchange Paul himself for an idea. Hence, in claiming to "have become all things to all people," Paul not so much "defends past actions"[76] as anticipates future readings. It would be better, I contend, to recognize the writer's arbitrariness and let it stand as it is, to thus thwart the either/or paradigm and allow opportunity for a twinkling of the Neutral to emerge.

---

[75] Christopher Poindexter, *Naked Human* (Mansfield, TX: Monarch Publishing, 2017), 34.
[76] Cf. Fee, *Corinthians*, 426, n. 21.

Earlier in 1 Corinthians, while addressing the various factions in the community and their divisiveness, the writer asks, "What is Paul?" (3:5). In so doing, he not only anticipates his fate in the history of reception, but also prefigures the Barthesean mode of self-narration characterized by *Roland Barthes by Roland Barthes*: "I am pigeonholed, assigned to an (intellectual) site, to residence in a caste (if not in a class). Against which there is only one internal doctrine: that of *atopia* (of a drifting habitation). Atopia is superior to utopia (utopia is reactive, tactical, literary, it proceeds from meaning and governs it)."[77] The tone of the question is one that borders on sarcasm,[78] one that hints at banality and resignation. It encapsulates both the shift from person to idea that takes place in the mythologization of Paul, and the characterization of the "I" as an Other that is the inevitable byproduct of the writing-self.

Weak

"The Neutral" should not be confused with the notion of "neither/nor." What Barthes terms "neither/nor criticism"[79] is a certain posture or presumption of objectivity. It is a faux-sense of neutrality that is driven by a naive and deceptive value system wherein terms like "culture" and "ideology" are juxtaposed one to the other so as to strike a balance. The "neither/nor" position stems from the *a priori* assumption that one can stand outside of the system in which such aforementioned terms operate. However, as Barthes points out, that position itself operates as one pole in another system of opposition. It, too, reflects an ideology. Hence, the Neutral represents an effort to break, abandon altogether, and render useless and meaningless the system of oppositions that create and enforce meaning.

---

[77] Barthes, *Roland Barthes*, 49. The writer's statement also prefigures the fragmentary condition of the speaker and the lover's monologue itself in *Lover's Discourse* through which Barthes attempts to present "the *love story*, subjugated to the great narrative Other, to that general opinion which disparages any excessive force and wants the subject himself to reduce the great imaginary current, the orderless, endless stream which is passing through him, to a painful, morbid crisis of which he must be cured, which he must 'get over'" (7; emphasis in original).

[78] Cf. Barthes, *Mythologies*, xii: "I don't share the traditional belief that there's a divorce in nature between the objectivity of the scientist and the subjectivity of the writer, as if the former were endowed with a 'freedom' and the latter with a 'vocation,' both of them likely to spirit away or sublimate the true limits of their situation: my claim is to live to the full contradiction of my time, which can make sarcasm the condition of truth."

[79] Ibid., 161–64.

The Neutral is not passionless. It is not neutral in the sense of objective, uncommitted, value-free.[80] Hence, I do not think the writer's posture in 1 Corinthians is one of disinterestedness. His statements do not sound to me like avoidance or indecision, nor do they seem driven by an outright lack of concern about what his readers think of him.[81] Instead, in the writer's deflection, I detect a degree of resistance to deciding between any two options, or among many, with an implicit invitation to his readers to think differently about him and thus also about themselves. It is a resistance to assignment, an anxiety about the violence necessitated by meaning. Interestingly, some earlier commentators caught a whiff of what is going on here. Orr and Walther state: "A believer in this gospel does not belong particularly to any group but can belong to all; so he is at home wherever he is and at the same time is a stranger even when he is at home."[82] This is indeed part of it. The writer aims to baffle a system and to circumvent any assignment or adoption of location that would impose an identity that is always and already secondary to the self. But in this final figure, "weak," we encounter something different, something that pushes beyond even what Orr and Walther conclude. "I became weak" is not an assertion of some true or essential self in opposition to a mistaken manifestation thereof, but an attempt to circumvent the self altogether.[83]

---

[80] "There is a passion of the Neutral but . . . this passion is not that of a will-to-possess" (Barthes, *The Neutral*, 13).

[81] To be sure, biblical interpreters identify a strong voice in this passage and throughout the letter, one taking a defensive stance against misinterpretation, no less. I, however, am not arguing for the same affirmation of the self over against misunderstanding on the part of the Corinthian readers that most exegetes see at work in the letter, but for a different sense of the self and of self-narration altogether.

[82] Orr and Walther, *1 Corinthians*, 243.

[83] Sampley, along with a number of other interpreters, connects the final statement to Paul's position concerning the practice of meat sacrificed to idols in 1 Corinthians 8. Despite Paul's own perspective on the matter and his own awareness of the freedom he has to conduct himself however he sees fit in relation to the consumption of meat dedicated to idols, he voluntarily identifies with the weak (i.e., those with scruples about such practices) and stands in solidarity with them, embodying an attitude of deference toward those who might otherwise take offense and falter in their faith due to conscience ("First Letter to the Corinthians," 908; cf. J. Paul Sampley, "The Weak and the Strong: Paul's Careful and Crafty Rhetorical Strategy in Romans 14:1–15:13," in *The Social World of the First Christians: Essays in Honor of Wayne A. Meeks*, eds. L. Michael White and O. Larry Yarbrough [Minneapolis: Fortress Press, 1995]), 40–52. In such readings, "weak" is substantive. It is an identity, and it is meaningful. Ironically, *weak* is transformed into something strong. Once again, the very effort to articulate and explicate what the writer is describing results in a move that violates and that does violence. The Neutral is neutralized. David Alan Black rejects the connection of "weak" in 1 Cor. 9:22 to the use of "weak" in 1 Corinthians 8. Because the writer's stated objective is that of "winning" (i.e., "saving") the weak, they must not already be converts (*Paul, Apostle of Weakness*, rev. ed. [Eugene, OR: Pickwick Publications, 2012], 75–77). What is most intriguing in Black's reading is that (i) "weak" is an umbrella term for Jews and Gentiles (i.e., everyone mentioned in the preceding verses), and (ii) his conclusion that "it seems better to modify somewhat the meaning of

The writer's turn to "weak" is a culminating stroke of the Neutral in the passage. The line that follows (viz., "I have become all things to all people") is not the conclusion but the denouement, a sort of aftereffect. It is a statement of outcome, the final reveal. It explains the result of the writer's effort to sidestep being strictly associated, pigeonholed, which is nothing other than his subsequent assignment by others to the myth that supplants him. It is an act whereby the writer gives in, or gives himself over. In order to circumvent the violence necessary for meaning, the writer abandons the paradigm, appealing to a Neutral term that baffles the system, at least potentially. In effect, the writer says, "I became meaningless," or rather, the "I" becomes meaningless, namely, in its subversion of connotation. The writer's "weakness" does not signify a failure or lack of strength, an alternative posture to strong. Rather, it reflects a drift toward an "epoch of rest," a "utopia of weariness."[84]

Violence, unfortunately, is inherent in language. The desire for meaning and the force of discourse will always threaten to stop the sliding, to silence the rustling, to fix the fluidity. Hence, it is the writer's weakness—both his unwillingness and his inability to assert meaning—that allows him to be co-opted and conscripted. It is the condition and the cure of all the adaptations that will proliferate, the almost limitless malleability and fecundity that interpreters of every ilk will shape into so many useful images, which are then presented as models for imitation. Despite its power to thwart any system that allows for meaning, the Neutral is fragile and precarious. Vulnerability is the alternative to violence.

The impetus for Barthes's course on the Neutral is a fantasy. He states at the outset: "This course: The Neutral or, better: 'The Desire for Neutral.'"[85] He says of the Neutral: "I am not trying to define a word; I am trying to name a thing."[86] Similarly, my goal in this chapter was not to define the Neutral in the passage, to fill an absence, to infuse it with meaning. I do not want to be guilty in my reading of 1 Cor. 9:19-23 of remythologizing Paul, or of

---

asthenēs than to give a completely different sense to *kerdainein*" (77). Black's analysis, first, suggests that Paul is somehow always either Jew or Gentile. Furthermore, it exemplifies perfectly Barthes's contention that meaning is enacted through violence by requiring the interpreter to choose between two opposing terms.

[84] See Rudolphus Teeuwen, "An Epoch of Rest: Roland Barthes's 'Neutral' and the Utopia of Weariness," *Cultural Critique* 80 (2012): 1–26.

[85] Barthes, *The Neutral*, 1.

[86] Ibid., 6.

substituting one assertion for another, or of presuming to have unlocked a secret. I have attempted, instead, to identify a glimmer of the Neutral in the passage, to capture a glimpse of the Neutral in the writer's discourse.[87] Remembering that the Neutral is a sort of fantasy is important. My reading is itself marked by fantasy. It stems from the desire for a nonviolent reading: one that neither mythologizes the author nor imposes meaning through decision and designation, one that prefers the rustle to the declaration, one that is not marked by a will-to-possess.

---

[87] Cf. Barthes's comments concerning the fragments that make up the content of his course: "fragment not of the Neutral but in which, more vaguely, there is some Neutral . . ." (*The Neutral*, 10).

4

The Disease of Paul

2 Corinthians 12:1-10 is a fascinating pericope that has served as fodder for much speculation. The writer's tantalizing description of a nameless someone "caught up to the third heaven," coupled with his reference to "a thorn in the flesh," which he further describes only in terms of an equally opaque characterization (viz., "a messenger of Satan"), has intrigued readers and commentators for generations, setting them to salivating over whether the writer is speaking of himself being enraptured, the nature of the secret revealed to the one transported, and the precise, tangible, "real" referent of that titillating thorn.

Fascination with this episode, in the writer's narrative of himself, and in this particular collage of images drawn from his image-repertoire, is striking for its range. James D. Tabor seems especially enthralled when he writes of the passage: "Here we have a precious bit of evidence of an actual *experience* of ascent to heaven from the early Roman imperial period. I emphasize the element of experience, because Paul's text is the only *firsthand* account of such a journey to heaven surviving from this period."[1] Commentators typically cite a long tradition of fascination, emendation, and elaboration vis-à-vis Paul's ascent, journey, time away, and the "third heaven," specifically. According to Tabor, "the early fathers had no problem with taking Paul at face value."[2] Dennis R. MacDonald, pointing out the general lack of interest in Paul's letters overall among the early Christian writers who composed narratives about him, notes that writers of Pauline apocalypses were quite drawn to 2 Cor. 12:1-4. Despite the writer's assertion that the revelations signified could not—perhaps, by

---

[1] James, D. Tabor, *Things Unutterable: Paul's Ascent to Paradise in its Greco-Roman, Judaic, and Early Christian Contexts* (Lanham, MD: University Press of America, 1986), 1.

[2] Ibid., 4.

implication, even should not—be expressed or articulated, these writers latched on to the suggestiveness and exploited the secrecy with verve. MacDonald lists as examples the now lost *Ascension of Paul*, the Gnostic *Apocalypse of Paul*, and the Catholic *Apocalypse of Paul*. According to MacDonald, there is a "translation of a reconstructed Latin version of the text [that] extends for some forty pages."[3] What is most intriguing for this book is the conclusion of this particular apocalypse: "I, Paul, came to myself and I knew and understood what I had seen and I wrote it in a scroll. And while I lived I did not have the time to reveal this mystery, but I wrote it (down) and deposited it under the wall of a house of that believer with whom I was in Tarsus, a city of Cilicia."[4] Meanwhile, what Robert D. Sider says of Tertullian's writings is equally applicable to both the autobiographical fragments in the New Testament letters and the subsequent interpretations of them by professional and causal readers alike:

> We should not expect to derive from the treatises of Tertullian a fully articulated biography of Paul; we have primarily allusions, frequently fleeting. These allusions appear to be motivated by two considerations. On the one hand, aspects of Paul's life have become the focus of debate, in cases with "heretics" but sometimes in debates within the church. On the other hand, many allusions, perhaps the majority, belong to the literary artifice of the treatises and have an essentially literary motivation, above all to provide illustrations and *exempla*.[5]

A variety of familiar themes surface in the excerpt from the reconstructed Latin apocalypse above: the implied signature, author, and authorization of the first-person voice; the return to the self and the subsequent reunification thereof; the contradiction (e.g., between one Paul who will not divulge what he has supposedly seen and heard, and another Paul who will not only disclose the secret but also do so with exposition); the affirmation of knowledge and understanding; the guarantor of writing; the trope of unavailable time; and the securing of the secret by means of hiding it again—though the security provided by that gesture is not one of protecting it from (re)discovery but of ensuring

---

[3] Dennis R. MacDonald, "Apocryphal and Canonical Narratives about Paul," in *Paul and the Legacies of Paul*, ed. William S. Babcock (Dallas: Southern Methodist University Press, 1990), 55–70, 56.
[4] Ibid., 56.
[5] Robert D. Sider, "Literary Artifice and the Figure of Paul in the Writings of Tertullian," in *Paul and the Legacies of Paul*, 99–120, ed. William S. Babcock (Dallas: Southern Methodist University Press, 1990), 100.

the retention, perpetuation, and persistence of its significance and connotation as a secret by effectively ordaining and determining that phenomenon of (re)discovery and the mythological functions associated with it.

To varying degrees, interpreters of 2 Corinthians credit the audience with determining the shape of the writer's construction of his self, for example, challenging his *authority*, taking pride in their Jewish heritage, boasting of particular accomplishments they deemed significant in the establishment of their own identity, and priding themselves on their extraordinary "visions and revelations." But, because he boasts in his weaknesses and therefore does not actually match the claims of his rivals, his boast parodies their boasts and, by extension, them as well.[6] "Over against the pretentious boasts of those who claim for themselves special apostolic powers and religious insights, Paul offers a long list of sufferings (11:23b-29) and the curious account of a journey to heaven which yielded no useful religious knowledge (12:1-4). This, as the apostle explicitly says in 11:30-33 and 12:5-10, is a boasting *of weakness.*"[7]

The trend among commentators to "wonder" if the Corinthians themselves had boasted of "visions and revelations"[8] in order to then read Paul's similar (but not identical) boast as a counter-boast that also supersedes (even as it acts as a gesture of dismissal) makes me "wonder" about the "significance" of the boast if the Corinthians had not. Does it effectively become meaningless in a different way (i.e., no longer meaningless in the writer's estimation but in ours)? Or does it become no longer a situation of "I could but I won't" and rather a more direct boast wherein the writer actually slips up, as it were, laying claim to something that most certainly does not signify weakness?

Interpreters tend to treat the entire passage in relation to the rhetorical handbooks such that Paul emerges as a well-trained and deft rhetorician:[9] a myth of Paul the literary elocutionist. To be sure, I recognize and appreciate the writer's use of form and techniques. After all, by what other means could he speak, given that form and technique are inherent in language? Nevertheless, I want to consider different aspects of form (e.g., the paradoxical over the

---

[6] Victor Paul Furnish, *II Corinthians: A New Translation with Introduction and Commentary* (Garden City: Doubleday & Company, 1984), 532–33 and 536.

[7] Furnish, *II Corinthians*, 533.

[8] See, e.g., J. Paul Sampley, "The Second Letter to the Corinthians: Introduction, Commentary, and Reflections," in *The New Interpreter's Bible*, vol. XI, 1–180 (Nashville: Abingdon Press, 2000), 162.

[9] See, e.g., Sampley, "Second Letter to the Corinthians," 155–56.

doxical), and to do so differently (e.g., identifying ways or moments in which form is used against itself, or turns back upon itself). There are five items of note in 11:22-33. First, the references in 11:22 to "Hebrews," "Israelites," and "descendants of Abraham." Second, the self-reflective exclamation in 11:23a, "I am out of my mind to speak this way" ("I am speaking like a madman" in the NRSV). Third, the catalog of hardships in 11:23b-28. Fourth, the appeal to "weakness" and to "the things that show [the writer's] weakness" in 11:29-30. And, finally, the escape from Damascus glossed in 11:32-33.

Although it occurs second in the order of the pericope, I want to begin with the writer's exclamation in 11:23a that he is speaking "like" a *paraphronon*, a madman, one who is out of his mind. The word signals a wandering from reason. In its verbal form, it means to be beside oneself. "Speaking" as it is used here carries the sense of prattling. The manner of the writer's speech is that of babbling; it is drivel. The two terms function together: to prattle is to feign or imitate madness, and to play the fool is to blather. With respect to matters of (auto)biography, this exclamation acts as a sort of punctum[10] in, through, and against the image-repertoire of the both the writer in reference to himself and any reader who would imagine the Author here made present by virtue of what precedes and follows, that is, as if he were writing *about* (himself) rather than actively writing (himself). As a punctum, it breaks the surface of the text, it speaks to us as directly as is possible (albeit still without speaking directly). If the writer is speaking *as if* a madman, then what we read is the madman. These are the words of a character being performed, but we cannot get behind the performance. The writer's interjection shatters the mirage. It reminds us of the writer's presence even as it draws attention to our inability to access it.

Second, the writer looks backward and begins by referencing a list of ethnic classifications (viz., "Hebrews," "Israelites," "descendants of Abraham"). They are marks of sociocultural identity, codes of location akin to what one finds in Phil. 3:4b-6. Were we to treat not only the letters of Paul as works (or together as a body of work, a corporeal corpus, thereby adding an additional layer of

---

[10] See Barthes, *Camera Lucida*. Barthes contrasts the *punctum* to the *studium*. The latter is akin to the *Doxa*. Barthes uses it to label that which draws us culturally, understandably to the subjects and aspects of a photograph. The *punctum*, on the other hand, is what interrupts the *studium* without being sought after. Barthes describes it as an "element which rises from the scene, shoots out of it like an arrow, and pierces" the viewer (26). A photograph's *punctum* is an accident that pricks, bruises, and is poignant to the viewer (27). Elsewhere, Barthes notes, "The *punctum* shows no preference for morality or good taste: the *punctum* can be ill-bred" (43).

signification), but also Paul himself (or rather perhaps the name of Paul itself, thereby recognizing and reinforcing the myth of Paul), these "incidents" in particular (though the same pertains differently to the "incidents" that follow in vv. 23b–28) would surely be incorporated into "a process of filiation."[11] Everything about them connotes origins, specification, identification, affinity: they are thus taken as signs of an Author and of an historical person. One would seek to index the ways in which Paul is determined by these things, but then also to explain how he is not, that is, how he distances himself from them and exceeds their limits, in order to individuate and appropriate him. But if we treat Paul as a text, we read him "without the Father's inscription."[12] In a manner analogous to treating 2 Corinthians as a letter and not a book, we might instead regard Paul-as-text as a network instead of considering Paul-as-work as an organism.

Third, save for its length, the list of troubles in 11:23b-28 is not unlike what one finds in Rom. 8:35; 2 Cor. 6:4c-5; 12:10 and to a lesser extent 1 Cor. 4:9-13. I would suggest that it also shares something in common with Phil. 3:4b-6 and 1 Cor. 9:20-22. Commentators typically refer to this list as a catalog, but a catalog connotes a sense of curation and purpose; it conjures a system. There is a randomness to this list; its arbitrariness and the seemingly offhanded manner in which it is recalled highlights the arbitrary and contrived nature of all lists, not to mention their inadequacy in representing the substance of a thing, not least of all the self.[13]

One might argue that they have a cumulative effect. One might argue, either also or alternatively, that they somehow allude to a narrative. Sampley insists: "Once again, hardships endured in the service of the gospel are Paul's best evidence and confirmation of his faithfulness and dependability with regard to the gospel and to the call to service. *Nothing* deters Paul."[14] He goes on to rave

---

[11] Barthes, "From Work to Text," 61.

[12] Ibid., 61.

[13] David Foster Wallace's review of *The Best of the Prose Poem* ("The Best of the Prose Poem" in *Both Flesh and Not*, 243–56) is a clever and insightful illustration of what I aim to note here. Composed and formatted as a series of sixty-seven bullet points that are equal parts superficial (e.g., the book's dimension, weight, word count), subjective (e.g., "other contributors, previously unknown to reviewer, who have good/alive/powerful/interesting pieces in anthology"), and sublime (e.g., "paradoxical consequence of above paradoxical problem for the 31 p.p.'s in the book that really are rich and alive and fine"), the "review" at once problematizes the form and function of both the book review genre and "the best of" genre, while also emphasizing the presence of the reader-reviewer as a writer in his own right.

[14] Sampley, "Second Letter to the Corinthians," 157; emphasis in original.

about the list itself, commenting on the excellence of its structure, the value of its content for confirming "some details already known about Paul" even while providing additional new information,[15] and the specific work the list performs: namely, the embrace of "shameful circumstances." Sampley's portrayal of the writer's embrace evokes a sense of affection and valuation. Paul's identification and solidarity with anyone who is weak is, according to Sampley, the "subtext" of the list.[16] This desire for an underlying theme, something other and greater than the writing itself, feeds directly into the mythification of Paul, but the character that evolves in that story is no longer identical to the one writing.

Barthes invites a reading against depth.[17] I get the sense that the writer of 2 Corinthians is talking around or in avoidance of something. Barthes offers the example of an "idle subject" who has "relaxed his image-repertoire" and allows his mind to wander, observing various things along his journey: "All these incidents are half identifiable: they issue from known codes, but their combinative operation is unique, it grounds the stroll in a difference which cannot be repeated except *as difference*. This is what happens in the Text: it can be Text only in its difference (which does not mean its individuality)."[18] I do not take Barthes to mean the same thing by "combinative operation" as "cumulative effect." While the latter suggests a teleology, the former evokes a rustling. Moreover, it seems to me that this list of hardships cannot signify at once both the life of Paul (i.e., it cannot function as autobiography and subsequently the raw materials of biography by later writers) *and* the values, meanings, significations attached to it in service to the mythification of Paul (e.g., endurance in service to the gospel, evidence and confirmation, faithfulness and dependability, call to service, and so on). To do so would be to imagine significance and meaning as self-evident and innate rather than ascribed.

My fourth observation concerns the writer's appeal to "weakness" and to "the things that show [the writer's] weakness" in 11:29-30. This is typically read as a sort of conclusion: the preceding list of things illustrates weakness,

---

[15] Cf. Furnish (*II Corinthians*, 537), who appeals to Acts noting that it does not provide any "actual portrayal" of Paul's beatings (save for Acts 16:22 by the Romans in Philippi) but also that it does not contradict what Paul is saying here insofar as it still depicts occasions prior to the writing of 2 Corinthians when they could have occurred.

[16] Sampley, "Second Letter to the Corinthians," 158.

[17] See Sontag, "Writing Itself," xxiii–xxv; cf. Barthes, "To Write: An Intransitive Verb."

[18] Barthes, "From Work to Text," p. 60; emphasis in original.

and the writer takes pride in his weakness (anticipating 12:5 and 9b-10). It represents the proverbial bottom line and reiterates by means of echoing 1 Cor. 9:22. "The genius of fools has always been in their freedom from convention," writes Sampley, "in their holding a lens through which we see what is not otherwise clear. In a subversion of the culture's value system—and perhaps also that of at least some Corinthians—weakness becomes Paul's badge of honor."[19] But if Paul becomes a genius in playing the fool, then nothing is upended. If weakness is a badge of honor, then the myth of honor has assimilated weakness. Not surprisingly, then, Sampley is quick to caution that this weakness "is not powerlessness; neither does it lead to Paul's withdrawal."[20] The writer says in v. 30: "I will boast of the things *that show* my weakness." That is different than boasting of one's weakness. Weakness, here, is a thing signified. But to whom?

According to Sampley, "Paul's resort to boasting in his weakness is not *simply* a strategical move in his struggle with the Corinthians; it is also and more profoundly his tapping of a fundamental truth of his life . . . Paul trusts in God's faithfulness and mercy and expects God to deliver. *That is the story of Paul's life and of the life of faith.*"[21] Indeed, it is not Paul's life; it is the *story of* Paul's life, which is then in turn transposed onto "the life of faith," which is not an actual life in any biological or biographical sense, but rather an *image-at-one's-disposal*; image and "thing" collapse into one: "Paul" is as we imagine and vice versa. The "life of faith" is imagined, read onto aspects of the myth that confirm it, and then reflected back to us as not only an example or illustration but as a directive.

Furnish argues that the point of the writer's rhetorical question in 11:29a ("Who is weak, and I am not weak?") is that "he so far identifies himself with those whom he serves as an apostle that their weaknesses are also his."[22] His comments suggest the possibility of weakness acting something like a

---

[19] Sampley, "Second Letter to the Corinthians," 158.

[20] Ibid., 158.

[21] Ibid., 160; my emphasis.

[22] Furnish, *II Corinthians*, 538. Furnish lists four possibilities for the meaning of "weak": (i) weak in conscience (e.g., 1 Cor. 8:7-13; cf. 10:24–11:1); (ii) weak in faith; (iii) "Christians who, for whatever reason, are less honored within the body of Christ," in which case what the writer says about himself in 2 Cor. 11:29 is a concrete "example of the operation of the principle enunciated in 1 Cor. 12:26a: 'If one member suffers, all suffer together'"; or (iv) physical weakness, viz., the "thorn in the flesh." The difference between the writer actually being weak and embracing weakness, on one hand, and the writer sharing in the weaknesses of others but in this case he himself not *necessarily* being weak per se or in the same way, on the other, is not insignificant.

contagion: the writer experiences an empathy so intense and extensive, so pervasive and all-encompassing that it becomes an identification with the (weak) Other, even with the weakness itself. At the same time, Furnish notes, in reference to 11:30 and elsewhere, that "the necessity of boasting makes it no less foolish."[23] Taken together, the writer's utterance of these impulses is analogous to Barthes's performance *A Lover's Discourse*. It is not the expression of the self that it might appear but rather borders on a total loss or erasure of the self, and with that perhaps gestures toward a radical reconceptualization of the self.

Indeed, with respect to Barthes, it is the necessity (e.g., of affinity with a perceived aspect of an Other or prompted by the perception of being forced to boast), in fact, stemming as it does from the determination, enforcement, imposition by others and by the system, a mythology of the self premised upon identity fashioned through conformity, that is foolishness. If we read the boast of weakness solely or merely as a counter-boast that elevates something otherwise shameful in order to invert a mythology of honor and shame or the like, as so many commentators seem wont to do, then the writer has gained nothing, and neither have we. Instead, we reinscribe the writer according to our own persistent systems of sociocultural classification.

Commentators like Furnish read the writer's list of troubles in 11:23b-29 "as documentation of how much he has suffered, and therefore of his vulnerability."[24] Hardships, personal characteristics, and behaviors combine to "disclose" an abstract principle: the revelation of God's power in weakness. This cannot be read as some new kind of power, or an alternative source of power, or the magical means by which one obtains power. It is an abolishment of power altogether. Disguised by "the illusion of expressivity," the surface of the text presents a vexation and weariness:

> As a writer, or assuming myself to be one, I continue to fool myself as to the *effects* of language: I do not know that the word "suffering" expresses no suffering and that, consequently, to use it is not only to communicate nothing but even, and immediately, to annoy, to irritate (not to mention the absurdity). . . . What writing demands, and what any lover cannot grant

---

[23] Ibid., 539.

[24] Ibid., 539. Elsewhere he states: ". . . this catalog of hardships is distinguished from those in 4:8-9 and 6:4c-5 by its greater length and specificity, giving it special value as an autobiographical statement" (536).

it without laceration, is to sacrifice *a little* of his Image-Repertoire, and to assure thereby, through his language, the assumption of a little reality.[25]

The only way to accomplish this, according to Barthes, is "to let [oneself] be subjected by [one's] language, submit to the injustices (the insults) it will not fail to inflict upon the double Image of the lover and of his other."[26] In the imagined rejection of the system altogether, the writer of 2 Corinthians gestures toward the Neutral. Weakness undercuts and nullifies power by being without asserting. Even divine power is undone, reconceived as powerlessness, for if God's power is made perfect in weakness it must itself be weakness of a sort. Similar to the way fascination and stupidity function as indivisible kernels of the self for Barthes, the (writing) self is inscribed in weakness for the writer of 2 Corinthians.

Finally, the writer's brief rehearsal of his escape from Damascus in vv. 32–33 appears to fit awkwardly with the material that surrounds it. It bears all the marks of an afterthought. To whatever extent it signifies anything, it does so differently and the thing it signifies is of a different sort (i.e., it appeals to or functions on the basis of a different code and operates on a different register) than the list of troubles that come before it. Furnish says that the verses "constitute a brief narrative account of a notable experience."[27] But what is notable about it? The emphasis seems to be on how *un*remarkable it is. The description, in fact, is rather banal considering what *seems* to be depicted and the sorts of things we so often associate with escape. Where is the risk and daring? Hence, Sampley notes: "Strikingly absent from the story is a single detail of anything Paul did or had to do in order to be delivered. There is no word of any plan or of specific co-conspirators, just the simple, powerful detail."[28] This "simple, powerful detail" is nothing other than a reality effect. But for someone like Sampley, the detail is "powerful" because it and the narrative of which it is a part connote a fundamental characterological identity that informs the biographical identity of the author.[29] But in the end,

---

[25] Barthes, *Lover's Discourse*, 98; emphasis in original.

[26] Ibid., 99.

[27] Furnish, *II Corinthians*, 540–41. Furnish rightly notes that the escape is highlighted rather than the seriousness of the threat or any suffering experienced in the process.

[28] Sampley, "Second Letter to the Corinthians," 160.

[29] Acts 9:23-25 recounts a story of the character Paul's escape that resembles the story the writer of 2 Corinthians narrates. However, rather than one confirming the other and thus allowing us to deduce and ascertain with an added degree of assuredness certain biographical facts of an historical

the escape from Damascus serves as an apt allegory for the vanishing self that quietly, uneventfully, unexpectedly descends and takes flight from those who would keep guard in order to seize it.

Visions and Revelations

Back again to boasting, the writer begins with the caveat that boasting is both necessary and pointless; it is without purpose because it is not gainful activity. Appealing to writers like Hermogenes and Plutarch, commentators give Paul a gold star for tempering the impropriety of his braggadocio by justifying it as a necessity and in the same breath upholding moral standards and social norms by recognizing its uselessness and futility. Paul threads the proverbial needle once again. The repetition regarding the necessity of boasting might also be considered a resistance to it, as if the writer were attempting to force himself (literally, his self) into it; it reflects reticence, aversion, even disgust, and perhaps the anticipation of regret premised upon a sense of imminent and inevitable failure.

If boasting is not beneficial, what is or would be? What benefit might one imagine or presume it offers that it in fact does not? The context suggests something of an operation of establishment. And yet both operation and outcome are plagued by instability; they depend upon there being a constant value associated with various things that are ultimately fluid and precarious, and they are susceptible to the possibility of being one-upped.

Being nonetheless "necessary"—his writing again effectively determined by something exterior, it is obligated and constrained; it is not internal or expressive; he can only write and operate from within the discourse that conscripts him—the writer appears to remonstrate against the falderal he perceives such things to be in relation to whatever alternative economy of significance he envisions instead. Hence, on one hand, he will boast only

---

life, the transtextual link only further highlights various operations of signification. On one hand, there is a "distinction between experience revived (as if, for example, from the child's point of view) and recalled (from the perspective of an adult narrator)" (Marcus, *Autobiography*, 4). On the other hand, there is the difference between the omniscient narrator of Acts externally focalizing the character of Paul and this event, and the letter writer internally focalizing himself and this event retrospectively as a character-narrator. Between Acts and the letters, "Paul" is a homonym.

about someone else who, nevertheless, does seem to have the upper hand on suitable things about which to boast, and on the other hand, he will boast on his own behalf only about that which would be perceived shameful by most standards: namely, his weaknesses. In other words, on the surface, the writer refuses to boast about things that would be desirable and offers instead a boast about that which is unattractive. But, as was the case earlier, this only inverts without deconstructing, much less replacing, that which lies at the heart of the problem.

The writer writes sparingly, sparsely, scantily of an Other he claims to know of who was caught up and who heard things that the writer cannot disclose, unrevealable revelations, unutterable utterances. The abrupt interruption of material and its equally swift conclusion leave behind "the barest shell of a description."[30] The writer who has been going on and on becomes taciturn and terse. So many tantalizing but unanswered questions emerge: By what manner did he ascend? What was the purpose of his journey? What did he see and hear? Was it even the writer who ascended? The naked description resonates with Barthes's "zero degree" writing,[31] *écriture* marked by the absence of that which would characterize it as literature and the product of an Author: "a product now divorced from the person and activity of its producer . . . the name for the coming to language of a knowledge which is not personal."[32] Reminiscent of free indirect discourse, it is insubstantial by design, the very essence of weak. What remains of both the journey and the aural revelation is only the writing, in which an effort is made to simultaneously write and unwrite, to say without saying, to sidestep expression. Despite the writer's repeated insistence that he does not know even the most basic detail of the experience (viz., whether or not it happened physically), most commentators regard the "person in Christ" that the writer claims to know as an indirect and veiled self-reference to the writer himself.[33] Although apparently not uncommon in antiquity, Furnish

---

[30] Paula R. Gooder, *Only the Third Heaven? 2 Corinthians 12.1-10 and Heavenly Ascent* (London: T&T Clark, 2006), 1.

[31] Roland Barthes, *Writing Degree Zero*, trans. Annette Lavers and Colin Smith (1953; New York: Hill & Wang, 1967).

[32] Ann Banfield, "Écriture, Narration and the Grammar of French," in *Narrative: From Malory to Motion Pictures*, ed. Jeremy Hawthorne (London: Arnold, 1985), 13; cited in Jeremy Hawthorne, *A Concise Dictionary of Contemporary Literary Theory* (London: Arnold, 1992), 54.

[33] Furnish notes that Betz (*Der Apostel Paulus und die sokratische Tradition. Eine exegetische Untersuchung zu einer "Apologie" 2 Korinther 10-13* [Tübingen: Mohr, 1972], 95) and Andrew T. Lincoln ("'Paul the Visionary': The Setting and Significance of the Rapture to Paradise in

notes that this is the only passage where it is used in the Pauline corpus.[34] Equating the writer with the ascendant resists the writer's resistance to the conflation, its connotation, and any capitulation to the constraints of a system wherein a phenomenon such as this counts for anything. What is not beneficial is, in part, not necessarily recounting the phenomenon of having *had* visions and revelations but the recounting of what they were, their content. Yet, even still, gesturing toward the experience, in this context, nevertheless refracts the inescapability of one's self being scripted and conscripted by terms that lie outside of it.

Despite the presumed uselessness that the writer ascribes to any description of the ascension experience beyond saying that it happened, the writer still uses it, and commentators who regard it as a parody in turn grant it an even greater usefulness in doing so.[35] Tabor suggests that what lies behind the scholarly consensus and contemporary approach to interpreting Paul and his letters is a tendency to "disparage such ecstatic experiences and [to maintain] that his journey to heaven had little or no connection with his message or his claim of

II Corinthians XII.1-10," *New Testament Studies* 25 [1979]: 208–9) suggest the possibility "that Paul has been moved to adopt this form [i.e., of using the third person to speak of the experience of being caught up] because he shares the conventional wisdom that it is better to praise another with whom one can expect to be compared (see 12:5) than to praise oneself directly (e.g., Plutarch, *On Praising Oneself Inoffensively* 10; Quintilian XI, 21)" (543–44). If so, then the pattern of playacting already witnessed in Roman 7 and 1 Corinthians 9 persists, but only if one already presumes to know a coherent and consistent self behind the mask, which is something the writer himself would seem reticent to claim on his behalf if this passage is any indication.

34   See, e.g., Furnish, *II Corinthians*, 542. Like Furnish, et al., Sampley does not regard Paul's use of the third person as anything other than a rhetorical maneuver designed to ward off accusations of self-aggrandizement. But what are the implications of this hedging once combined with the sort of hedging (as described by Furnish via Plutarch or whomever re: the escape from Damascus) already at work in the writer's self-deprecation through emphasizing his weakness(es)? Where is the self, if neither in the experience of revelation nor in the marks of inadequacy?

35   See, e.g., For Furnish, *II Corinthians*, 543; Cf., Keener, *1–2 Corinthians*, 237, who contends that the writer is not parodying the ascension narrative but only boasting. I do not think the dismissal of significance leads necessarily to parody or that reading it as parody goes far enough. If the writer is parodying boasting, then even his weakness is rendered void and meaningless. It is employed solely in service to comedic effect. But to whatever extent this is achieved, weakness seems to function as something that thwarts the system more fundamentally. Cf. Gooder, *Only the Third Heaven?*, 195: ". . . while I seek to uphold the general sense of Betz's argument that the Pauline account of ascent is designed to subvert the Corinthian understanding of true apostleship, it seems difficult to use the term parody of the account in the technical sense. . . . The account in 2 Corinthian 12 seems to record too genuine an experience to suggest technical parody of ascent. Nevertheless, it does seem to contain an element of subversion. While various motifs readily suggest a connection with the genre of heavenly ascent, the account is so terse and contains such little detail that it stands out as extremely unusual. On closer examination it seems that the enigmatic account tells the story of a failed, not a successful, ascent. The element of subversion is two-fold. On the one hand accounts of failed ascents are not normally recounted and on the other Paul not only narrates it but boasts about it."

apostolic authority," which is based on interpretations of 2 Corinthians 10–13 that "set Paul against his opponents at Corinth, claiming that his theology of the cross, and his emphasis on suffering, run contrary to any cultivation of ecstatic experiences of revelation."[36]

Tabor pursues a fascinating array of questions concerning "the heavenly journey" motif in antiquity (e.g., the type of journey, the type of text reporting the journey—and here, Paul's account is singled out as a "rare example of an identifiable, autobiographical account"—the signification of the narrated experience), and concludes that "ascent to heaven is a *characteristic* expression of Hellenistic piety, and as such is related to a relatively widespread set of shared perceptions."[37] The emphasis is placed, once again, on matters of form and convention, reiterating the overt molding of the self in conformity to something that precedes it, that is external to it, and that signifies peripherally something other and more effective than the content it appears to deliver. Despite Tabor's thick description of the context and his effort to take what is said "at face value," to take the writer "at his word," he does not get us any closer to "Paul" or to Paul's "life" because whether I take his words at face value or try instead to see past them, whether I read the words in relation to an ancient context or a modern one, whether or to whatever extent I imagine some degree of separation between content and (rhetorical) form, I am no less confronted with the undecidability of the writer's image-repertoire, which is further compounded by my own, and myth's process of overtaking the historical body thereby unfolds.

Barthes offers an example in "Myth Today" that I think illustrates what is happening at the level of both the writer and the reader.

If I am a woodcutter and I am led to name the tree which I am felling, whatever the form of my sentence, I "speak the tree," I do not speak about it. This means that my language is operational, transitively linked to its object; between the tree and myself, there is nothing but my labor, that is to say, an action. This is a political language [contra the depoliticized language of

---

[36] Tabor, *Things Unutterable*, p. 4. He goes on to say that "it is assumed, because Paul is Paul (i.e., great Christian theologian and apostle), he is somehow 'pure' of the magical-mystical elements associated with ascent to heaven in other materials of the period. . ." (4). Whether or not this is the specific assumption underlying the consensus view, I agree that a certain conception of Paul precedes and is subsequently read into the letters we claim as our primary source for knowing Paul.

[37] Ibid., 57 and 58.

myth]: it represents nature for me only inasmuch as I am going to transform it, it is a language thanks to which I *act the object*; the tree is not an image for me, it is simply the meaning of my action.[38]

The writer signals at least the desire for a language that does not speak about but only acts the object. It is not absent of meaning but it resists connotation and signification. At the level of the reader, however, it is an act of transformation whereby an "image-at-one's disposal" is produced.

I find the writer's mention of "fourteen years ago" one of the most curious details of all. Such precision would seem to lend the account a degree of importance and to validate or reinforce the writer's authenticity and trustworthiness. It reflects a pointedly historical (and thus autobiographical) interest in that it both happened and happened in the writer's past. The designation of time evokes prophetic pronouncement, apocalyptic discourse, the strange and unusual, and the gravitas of history.[39] Therefore, the designation also functions as a reality effect in that it marks the reality of this otherwise surreal and alternate reality that characterizes it, which is the very nature of "visions and revelations" and of ecstatic, enraptured experience. But critics cannot resist the temptation to make of it much more than that insofar as it becomes a datum for crafting a chronology of Paul's life and letters. To be sure, some will urge caution. For example, Furnish writes: "That Paul bothers to date it at all is not to be attributed to any special autobiographical or historical interests, but . . . to an interest in emphasizing that it really happened."[40] But even he proceeds to reconstruct a chronology in the very next sentence. Given that history does not signify on its own, the beauty of the timestamp is its undecidability: it is neither wholly meaningless nor wholly meaningful; neither insignificant nor significant. It oscillates in a space between, specifying not *when* but simply *that* this happened.

The writer *twice* contends that he does not know whether this individual was caught up in the body or out of the body. As far as the writer is concerned, only God knows. "God knows" signals both unknowability *and* factuality, certainty, that is, that there is still no less something, some matter of actual fact,

---

[38] Barthes, "Myth Today," 58; emphasis in original.

[39] See Furnish, *II Corinthians*, 544. Furnish cites Ezek. 1:1-3; 3:16; 8:1; Amos 1:1; Hos. 1:1; Isa. 6:1; Jer. 1:1-3; 26:1; Zech. 1:1; 7:1; 2 Esdras 3:1; 2 Apoc Bar 1:1; and Lucian, *The Lover of Lies* 11 and 22.

[40] Ibid., 544.

to be known, though it is accessible and perhaps even comprehensible only to an omniscient "God." But all that the writer claims to actually know, the only knowledge he claims to *possess*, is that someone was caught up into Paradise and heard things. He cannot even say whether the experience took place in or out of the body because it is the experience of an Other, of someone he knows only as an Other. Tabor insists that "we must take Paul's statement at face value. This journey to Paradise was something he experienced."[41] But actually doing so would require us to permit the writer to say nothing regarding the heavenly journey, to accept that the one of whom he speaks is *not* himself, and then to grant no significance to such an experience and its recounting. Like Barthes, the writer seems to say, "I cannot *write myself*. What, after all, is this 'I' who would write himself?"[42]

Attributing to the writer a *feigned* ignorance, and then attributing to it the function of signifying that the writer simply does not care (despite and in contrast to any concern his audience might have), serves the myth of "Paul" as one who is able to somehow imitate or speak the language of a group with which he does not identify convincingly enough that they will remain tuned in, listening, responsive, thinking he is speaking (on) their terms, but to do so *without* actually being one of them. Somehow his core identity, his essence, his self, which is paradoxically both wholly contextual and wholly anomalous (to use Bird's classification), remains "pure" insofar as it is unsullied by implicitly clearly defined boundaries of various alternative identities ("Jewish," "Gnostic," et al.). It is important to clarify that I do not mean Paul's individuality is maintained; rather, it is his *uniqueness* that is upheld and protected.

Paradoxically, the unsullied self that is championed in such a reading requires a bifurcated self. Although Furnish speaks of a "distance . . . between himself as narrator and the person whose journey to Paradise he has been describing,"[43] he does not mean that the writer is actually speaking about someone else as he states, much less see this as a condition of the self that marks it as fragmented and as a consequence of writing the self. Rather, it is viewed as the opposite: another instance of Paul escaping identification and association with whatever

---

[41] Tabor, *Things Unutterable*, 121.
[42] Roland Barthes, *A Lover's Discourse*, 98; emphasis in original.
[43] Furnish, *II Corinthians*, 546.

significance others might place on such an experience.[44] Therefore, Furnish distinguishes between the writer's "private self" for which he will lay claim to an experience like those his readers presumably boasted of having had, and his "public self" that concerns his apostolic status, which will only be established on the grounds of weaknesses (viz., the ignominious flight from Damascus and the "thorn").

The writer says he does not know the substance of what this individual heard but describes the quality and category referring to them as things "that are not to be told, that no mortal is permitted to repeat." They are secrets and mysteries, what he referred to earlier as "visions and revelations of the Lord." The substance of what cannot be divulged is oxymoronic. The otherworldly traveler heard "unutterable words" (*arrēta rēmata*) that no human being has permission or potential to voice. That the words *could* but *should not* be expressed because it would be unlawful to do so[45] begs the question of how law determines and enforces the prohibition. Moreover, one must consider that the writer effectively circumvents or violates any such impermissibility by writing into the void, as it were. Readers are inclined to grant a certain weight, a gravitas, to the unutterable utterances the writer writes only about and around, but in terms of function and in relation to the writer's self they are really no different than the "other things" not mentioned in 11:28 insofar as they gesture toward, without naming, them. The ambiguity and indeterminacy are critical, not least of all because the writer pointedly distinguishes between the one on whose behalf he will boast and himself (i.e., refusing to boast on his own behalf, "except of my weaknesses").

The words, *arrēta rēmata*, have a double connotation: they are associated with secrecy and inexpressibility, and this double connotation is compounded by the writer's claim that the words cannot be repeated or relayed. But something is not kept secret because it is inexpressible. Were it simply inexpressible, there would be no secret to keep; nothing need be kept because it is not possible to give it in the first place. On the other hand, if there is a secret, then its inexpressibility is governed not by the impossibility of expression but by something else, whether it be prohibition, or taboo, or desire, or

---

[44] "While [Paul] is quite willing to record this one instance of a private religious experience, he is quite unwilling to claim it as an apostolic credential" (ibid., 544).
[45] Tabor, *Things Unutterable*, 122; Furnish, *II Corinthians*, 526–27.

rhetorical purpose and function. In *The Pleasure of the Text*, Barthes describes pleasure as that which "can be expressed in words" as opposed to bliss which is "unspeakable."[46] What we encounter in 2 Cor. 12:2-4 is a text of bliss. It is foremost a text of bliss on the part of the writer, but it can be a text of bliss for the reader also if we resist the urge to transform it into a text of pleasure.

"Paradise" is a utopian space, and here that utopia is characterized by an absenting of the self from this world by the suspension of language. What is experienced there cannot be spoken; the utopia of paradise itself can only be spoken *about*, not spoken *from* or *within*. Moreover, the writer's inability or refusal to say if it was in the body (and therefore Jewish) or out of the body (and therefore Greek)[47] characterizes the utopia of Paradise as an *atopia*, an unidentifiable, unassimilable, uncategorizable space between various "ideas," "ideologies," and "identities" to which we would assign the writer in resistance to his indeterminate and thus Neutral writing.

Some commentators have spoken of the significance of the ascent in terms of the failure(s) of Paul. For Tabor, it is tied to the dashed hopes following the destruction of the Temple, the crushed dream of bringing "Israel to accept Jesus as Messiah through his Gentile mission," and the miscarriage of his narrative and vision in the years following his death.[48] Paula R. Gooder identifies a theme of failure within the description itself, and notes the curious way in which this passage elicits what I would describe as disease, distraction, and desire.

Gooder is most of all concerned with the fact that the description of this ascent seems to be out of line with the flow of thought preceding and following it. The writer has been making a case against boasting of the things others deem meaningful in favor of boasting of weakness, but everything about this scene appears to be a matter of success. Hence, after identifying a rich tapestry of similarities and difference between the account in 2 Corinthians and numerous extracanonical parallels, and taking the latter as an indication of the writer's critical relationship with a tradition of heavenly ascent portraits demonstrated through various omissions and modifications, Gooder argues that the passage is best understood as a failure, and thus serves as another

---

[46] Barthes, *Pleasure*, 21.
[47] See Furnish, *II Corinthians*, 525.
[48] Tabor, *Things Unutterable*, 125.

example of weakness in the context of others. Arguing that Paul is working "on the basis of a seven-layered cosmology," she contends that "an ascent to the third with no subsequent ascent into higher levels of heaven certainly suggests some element of failure."[49] Her conclusion is that "either Paul reached the throne of God and did not mention it or he did not and this affects the telling of the event here."[50]

Gooder makes an important insight that one could extend beyond 2 Corinthians 12 to other autobiographical statements I am reading in this book. "One of the problems for scholars in interpreting this passage," she writes, "is how to make sense of the language in the passage. Images of 'visions' and 'revelations'; 'third heaven' and 'paradise'; 'being caught up' and 'hearing ineffable things' *do not fit easily in traditional interpretations* of Paul."[51] Because the topic and character of the text appear to be anomalous vis-à-vis the body of writing deemed authentically Pauline, "the imagery used requires explanation, but such an explanation cannot be found within the Pauline corpus itself."[52]

Among other things, Barthes was drawn to that which did not fit the system, to that which thwarted the system. It went by various names (e.g., the novelistic, the Neutral, the *paradoxa*). His interest was not in modifying the system in order to assimilate the ill-fitting datum but to draw attention to the arbitrariness of systems, to their inherent failure and limitation, and to the force they exert on the subjects they purport to name and classify. In the concluding figure of *A Lover's Discourse*, Barthes speaks of the lover's "ceaseless desire to appropriate the loved being in one way or another." Recognizing that it is not enough to abandon the "will-to-possess" if doing so means actively exhibiting the "non-will-to-possess," he concludes:

> For the notion of [non-will-to-possess] to be able to break with the system of the Image-repertoire, I must manage . . . to let myself drop somewhere outside

---

[49] Gooder, *Only the Third Heaven?* 191. Cf. C. R. A. Morray-Jones, "Paradise Revisited (2 Cor 12:1-12): The Jewish Mystical Background of Paul's Apostolate. Part 1: The Jewish Sources," *HTR* 86 (1993): 177–217; idem., "Paradise Revisited (2 Cor 12:1-12): The Jewish Mystical Background of Paul's Apostolate. Part 2: Paul's Heavenly Ascent and Its Significance," *HTR* 86 (1993): 265–92.

[50] Ibid., 191–92.

[51] Ibid., 8; my emphasis.

[52] Ibid., 8. She later notes that "almost all the scholars who have examined this passage have assumed that the only possible interpretation is that Paul did indeed reach the highest heaven" (190), which suggests an ideology at work: the myth of Paul precedes and overrides the statements of the writer, and the writer is conformed to the image-repertoire of his interpreters.

of language, into the inert, and in a sense, quite simply, *to sit down*. . . . not to try to possess the non-will-to-possess; to let come (from the other) what comes, to let pass (from the other) what goes; to possess nothing, to repel nothing: to receive, not to keep, to produce without appropriating, etc.[53]

In the end, even Gooder concedes that whether Paul is stressing weakness or parodying the ascent genre and the value others assigned to such experiences he is demonstrating his true apostolic identity by linking the failure to a prophetic tradition of affliction characterizing a genuine prophet.[54] Furnish takes the writer's insistence on what actually can be seen and heard by his readers as an indication that "his apostleship cannot be demonstrated by a recitation of his otherworldly experiences, but only the effectiveness of his this-worldly service as an apostle."[55] I am not convinced we get anywhere if we elevate weakness or some set of things such that they now count for more. Instead, I read on the writer's part a desire "to sit down," as it were, neither give in to the will-to-possess nor strategically employ the non-will-to-possess,[56] for the only way weakness and suffering might be genuinely effective is in their ineffectiveness. The writer's unassertive auto(bio)graph seems pointedly at odds with so many arguments that emphasize the writer's supposed efforts to assert apostolic status and authority.

Thorn and Consternation

The writer now shifts his attention from the past to the present, from an upward orientation to a lateral orientation, and from an Other to his own body. He makes reference to the "exceptional character of the revelations." What makes them exceptional? They are excepted from speech by virtue of their ineffability and unrepeatability. The revelations are the stuff of hyperbole (*tē hyperbolē*,

---

[53] Barthes, *Lover's Discourse*, 232–34; emphasis in original.
[54] Cf. Keener, *1-2 Corinthians*, 238, for whom "visions" signifies that Paul is a "biblical prophet."
[55] Furnish, *II Corinthians*, 546.
[56] "And if the [non-will-to-possess] were a tactical notion. . .? If I still (though secretly) wanted to conquer the other by feigning to renounce him? If I withdrew *in order* to possess him more certainly? The reversi (that game in which the winner takes the fewest tricks) rests on a feint familiar to the sages ('My strength is in my weakness'). This notion is a ruse, because it takes up a position within the very heart of passion, whose obsessions and anxieties it leaves intact" (Barthes, *Lover's Discourse*, 233; emphasis in original).

translated as "abundance" in the RSV and as "exceptional character" in the NRSV). Furnish glosses it with phrases such as "beyond any comparison," "absolutely incomparable," and "something which cannot be surpassed."[57] It suggests a sense of extravagance and is conceptually rooted in the notion of overshooting, passing beyond, or exceeding something. It is that which outmaneuvers the limits of language.

Just as the writer's self has been conditioned by and conformed to the discourse of his audience, so now it will by shaped by a different determinant: namely, a "thorn" that checks his self-exaltation.[58] Craig Keener succinctly summarizes the plethora of proposals concerning the identity of the thorn by grouping them into three categories: moral or psychological temptations; a physical ailment; or opponents of various sorts.[59] Furnish, meanwhile, attending to the rhetorical function of the writer mentioning the thorn, references "Philo's interpretation of the affliction visited upon Jacob (see Gen. 32:25)—that when the soul attains power and perfection it must be saved from conceit by a certain disablement (*Dreams* I, 130-31)"—and "Plutarch's advice that self-praise is rendered more palatable if one includes a reference to some personal flaw (*On Praising Oneself Inoffensively* 13)."[60] Hence, the

---

[57] Furnish, *II Corinthians*, 528.

[58] "Thorn (*skolops*) in the flesh" is an *hapax legomenon* (although "[in] the flesh" is exceedingly common in "Paul's" letters). At its most basic, it refers to "anything pointed, especially pale, stake" (LSJ), but it has been used to refer to an object for impaling, the point of a fishing-hook, and even an instrument for operating on the urethra. In Georg Autenrieth's *A Homeric Dictionary for Use in Schools and Colleges*, the word is defined as "a stake for impaling." Note also Num. 33:55 (LXX) "But if you do not drive out the inhabitants of the land from before you, then those whom you let remain shall be as barbs in your eyes and thorns in your sides; they shall trouble you in the land where you are settling." Coupled with the writer's statement regarding the perceived purpose of the "thorn"/"messenger of Satan" (viz., "to torment me"), the metaphor clearly evokes a sense of violence.

[59] Keener, *1-2 Corinthians*, 240; cf. Furnish, *II Corinthians*, 548-49: (i) personal anxiety or spiritual affliction; (ii) physical or mental illness; and (iii) persecution. According to Gooder, Barclay organized the possibilities into eight categories: spiritual temptation, opposition and persecution, carnal temptation, physical appearance, epilepsy, headaches, eye trouble, and malaria, which she then reduces to three major areas: a physical ailment, spiritual torment, and opposition or persecution (Gooder, *Only the Third Heaven?* 196–97). Speaking in the most general terms, Sampley ("Second Letter to the Corinthians," 162) regards the heavenly journey and the thorn in the flesh together as representative of "the extremes a person may experience in life," thereby imposing a frame that limits the limitless and the metaphorical.

[60] Furnish, *II Corinthians*, 547. For a very different take on the episode of Genesis 32, see Roland Barthes, "The Struggle with the Angle: Textual Analysis of Genesis 32:22-32," in idem. *Image-Music-Text*, 125–41 (1971). Barthes concludes by suggesting that "metonymic logic is that of the unconscious. Hence it is perhaps in that direction that one would need to pursue the present study, to pursue the reading of the text—its dissemination, not its truth. . . .The problem, the problem at least posed for me, is exactly to manage not to reduce the Text to a signified, whatever it may be (historical, economic, folkloristic, or kerygmatic), but to hold its *significance* fully open" (141; emphasis in original).

thorn, whatever it may be, simultaneously indicates an actual ailment (even if not physical)—a condition, weakness, disease—resulting from the writer's experience, and a stylistic device employed in service to a certain posture. As the argument goes, the "thorn" is a metaphor that could point to any of the aforementioned things or to something else altogether and its purpose was to keep Paul humble. God allowed it—gave it even—in a manner that evokes the story of Job. But the thorn meant to keep him humble paradoxically makes him even greater. Moreover, it is probably good we do not know what it is *so that* its ambiguity allows it to be applicable to any difficulty we face. Hence, the "thorn in the flesh" has become a commonplace idiom, a clever turn of phrase providing a cipher for anything and anyone that ails or aggravates, for whatever they might deem to be an obstacle, something to account for the lack of things that they might otherwise boast about. The thorn becomes overburdened and overdetermined, a sign capable of absorbing virtually anything and everything. But unlike Barthes's Eiffel Tower, in which he found a perfect sign characterized by its ability to be and mean everything,[61] the writer's thorn is a distraction: not a serendipitous or pleasurable diversion but a thing that *preventatively opposes from* and that also *agitates* the reader who would insist on ascertaining the revelation the writer himself refuses to unveil.

I have no interest in making one more guess as to the thorn's identity. I want to resist the allure of enticing shiny objects like the writer's unspeakable divine disclosures and thorny metaphors. My concern is the writer's self and his writing of his self. Whether or not we equate the one caught up to the third heaven with the one given the thorn in the flesh, the thorn becomes in some way representative of the burden of revelation, the weight of language, the heaviness of unutterable utterances. In its role as messenger (*aggelos*), it shuttles between the sender and the writer who identifies himself as "messenger" (*apostolos*), in

---

[61] See Roland Barthes, "The Eiffel Tower," (1964) in Sontag, *A Barthes Reader*, 199–211; cf., Sontag, "Writing Itself," xx–xxi: "By so extending the reach of meaning, Barthes takes the notion over the top, to arrive at such triumphant paradoxes as the empty subject that contains everything, the empty sign to which all meaning can be attributed. With this euphoric sense of how meaning proliferates, Barthes reads that 'zero degree of the monument,' the Eiffel Tower, as 'this pure—virtually empty—sign' that (his italics) '*means everything*.' (The characteristic point of Barthes's arguments-by-paradox is to vindicate subjects untrammeled by utility: it is the uselessness of the Eiffel Tower that makes it infinitely useful as a sign, just as the uselessness of genuine literature is what makes it morally useful.)" Stafford's summation of the Eiffel Tower in Barthes's semiological analysis certainly applies equally well to the thorn in Paul's flesh: "it attracted reactions and meanings like a lightening conductor" (*Phenomenon and Myth*, 85).

order to buffet the writer. The violent abuse that the writer describes echoes the self-pummeling of 1 Cor. 9:27 and the desperate dissatisfaction with the body of death in Rom. 7:24. In the writing-self, language, flesh, and body intersect and converge. Barthes characterized "language—the performance of a language system—[as] neither reactionary nor progressive; it is quite simply fascist; for fascism does not prevent speech, it compels speech."[62] The writer of 2 Corinthians is burdened and beset by the compulsion to at once speak and be silent, and he occupies that juncture in the space of writing.

If the writer and the visionary are one and the same, then this "gift" is a consequence of the journey, a reminder of the danger he faced, encountered, escaped, and was spared.[63] Despite having been "caught up"—a passive experience, beyond his control, not the result of his own doing or the outcome of his own search—he nonetheless violated a boundary, a taboo. But what is the justification for reading the "I" and "the man" as synonymous? To be sure, it is not difficult to read it as a rhetorical strategy. The writer, so fully intent on not boasting about having received visions and revelations of the Lord while in the latter's very presence in the "third heaven," chooses to distance himself from it by claiming no firsthand knowledge. "I do not know," according to Furnish, either accentuates Paul's uncertainty or his indifference.[64] But given that this is not what the text actually says, reading it this way betrays something on the part of the reader. To read seamlessly and without pause the split and differentiation in v. 5 in order to equate the "I" and "the man" is to allow the writer to put forward and then to retract, to withdraw, to "humble brag," as it were. Such a reading projects a unity, a coherency onto the writer's self, rather than recognizing the inherently fragmentary nature of the self, which is more appropriately imagined as a bricolage, a pastiche; the literary, writing, writerly self is a fiction, a plasma-like substance that is fabricated. It is neither the sum

---

[62] Roland Barthes, "Inaugural Lecture, Collège de France," in Sontag, *Roland Barthes Reader*, 461.

[63] See Keener, *1–2 Corinthians*, 238.

[64] Furnish, *II Corinthians*, 525. Equating the writer with "the man" about whom he writes, Keener describes the writer's uncertainty about whether he was in the body or out of it as a "rhetorical *aporia* (feigned uncertainty)" (Keener, *1–2 Corinthians*, 238). He goes on to say, "but Paul has already contrasted being at home in the body with the afterlife of being away from the body and at home with the Lord (5:6-8)," and I would add Phil. 1:21-24. Therefore, Keener takes the latter to warrant against the former. I am inclined to take the writer at his word, and also to combine the uncertainty with the indifference: the writer utters no desire to know. In speaking of himself as an Other, he recognizes the limits of self-knowledge and of self-writing, exposing a fissure, a cleavage, a contradiction, in the process.

of its parts nor something greater than the sum of its parts, but the tension and all that accompanies it.

Michael Goulder identifies four "uncomfortable hypotheses" involved in identifying the writer with the one transported to Paradise: (i) it was a convention to praise others rather than oneself; (ii) Paul distances himself because he is unwilling to claim charismatic experiences in support of his apostleship; (iii) Paul is distinguishing between his natural and spiritual selves; and (iv) "ascent into heaven involves transformation into the likeness of the divine Glory: the 'man in Christ' is Paul's transformed self."[65] The very danger that such claims of visual revelation present (and thus why they were forbidden) is precisely what someone like Sampley valorizes: "In Paul's culture, heavenly journeys often functioned to confirm divine approval and authentication. This story counts as a boast on that basis. By telling it, Paul obliquely claims special status for himself, a status so grand that his opponents might not be able to compete."[66]

The distinction Barthes makes between figuration and representation is useful here. The former "is the way in which the erotic body appears (to whatever degree and in whatever form that may be) in the profile of the text. For example, the author may appear in his text. . ., but not in the guise of biography (which would exceed the body, give a meaning to life, forge a destiny)." In contrast, "representation . . . is *embarrassed figuration*, encumbered with other meanings than that of desire: a space of alibis (reality, morality, likelihood, readability, truth, etc.)."[67] The reading of Sampley and others is one in which the writer functions as a representation that results in a text of pleasure, but it is "a *figure* of the text [that is] necessary to the bliss of reading."[68]

The writer does not desire to boast, and he claims to refrain from it, desiring instead to limit others' interpretation of him to nothing more than, nothing better than, what is seen in him or heard from him. It is easy to see here another familiar rhetorical maneuver: professing to not say something but saying it anyway, albeit indirectly. But what the writer marks in the saying-

[65] Michael Goulder, "Vision and Knowledge," *JSNT* 56 (1994): 54–55. He demonstrates that these arguments do not hold water largely because the parallels cited in support of them are not exact matches (see 54–58).
[66] Sampley, "Second Letter to the Corinthians," 163.
[67] Barthes, *Pleasure*, 55–56.
[68] Ibid., 56.

without-saying is not the thing (not) said but the weakness, the impotence of language vis-à-vis the self and his desire for it. Just as earlier the thing signified was not the things heard but the rustling of revelation, the writer of 2 Corinthians resists both denotations and connotations that would make visions, revelations, and proper boasts conduits of knowledge and guarantors of authority. The assumption that the weakness is something to be seen and heard presumes something external, whether physical or sociocultural (e.g., negotiations of hierarchy and status), and it accepts the terms of scale and definition in play among the Corinthians, that is, that they who, in the writer's view, already have misperceptions about the things that "count" are by those standards able to identify the writer's life (or whatever) as weak. Never minding that the writer and his audience appear to be engaged in a rhetorical bout over a trivial matter, there is a gesture toward something Neutral and in it an effort to offer or construct the self, a refraction of the writer's self, that is withdrawn and withdrawing, vanishing. The apparent assertion is a chimera. To latch hold of "Paul" in response to the apparition of avowal is either to miss or to outright abandon the writer. The commonplace tendency among commentators to cite numerous parallels in the rhetorical handbooks of the day and to various schools of philosophy purports to understand Paul in relation to his context. Yet, there is an equally persistent refusal to say that he is entirely the product of a context, be it ancient or modern. The reconstructed and historicized Paul goes hand in glove with the myth of Paul. The writer is conditioned, acclimated to form; he is conformed.

Any tendency to read the writer's boast, in any way or to any degree, as more legitimate, more noble, less arrogant, more valid, is a function of reading from a position already within the argument, that is, both taking him at face value and already assuming his position is the correct one. More importantly for the purposes of my reading, it is to view both the letter and its reading *not* as factors in the ongoing, active construction of the writer but as an expression, an extension, a projection of a self who already exists beforehand and independently of writing. Paul is regarded as a thinker and his letters as representative his thought. He is not a writer but an Author, not a literary character but a real person.

The writer indicates that he thrice asked the Lord "that it would leave [him]." According to Furnish, the appeal "shows, on the one hand, how intent he was on being helped and, on the other hand, that this is a request he no longer makes."[69] What, then, does the cessation of request signify? The writer indicates that the response he received was one of denial and reassurance: "My grace is sufficient for you, for power is made perfect in weakness." The repeatability of these words characterizes them as fundamentally different from the unutterable words heard by the one caught up into Paradise. They are presented neither as reported speech nor as free indirect speech but as a direct quote of words spoken to the writer, the only place in his letters where he makes such a claim. Is this not also a revelation? The difference is that this disclosure diverts: it is the stuff of appeasement and redirection. Returning then to the question concerning the meaning of the writer's discontinuance, his response ("So, I will boast all the more gladly of my weaknesses") seems to suggest resignation and acceptance, and that is certainly how interpreters read it. But this transforms the meaning and function of the thorn from a preventative measure to a palpable pleasure. Indeed, the writer emphasizes that it is with utmost pleasure (*hēdista*) that he will boast. The writer references such pleasure on only one other occasion, which happens to occur just six verses later when he says he would most pleasurably "spend and be spent" for his readers. There is a drift from something experienced to something interpreted. The thorn becomes a paradoxical source of comfort; it mollifies and placates; it possesses a conciliatory and soothing quality. To be sure, the words quoted by the writer earlier suggest that it is grace performing these functions, acting as supplement and salve to the prick that has punctured our protagonist. But all of this is the language and product of a retrospective reassessment, which Brian Price has argued is a political operation of regret. In the end, the thorn lingers. Reflecting on a passage in *Roland Barthes by Roland Barthes* wherein Barthes speaks, in third person, of his own regrets, Wilson writes: "What Barthes acknowledges in himself . . . is what he also has gotten over, since Barthes . . . sees something else than what 'he' once saw."[70]

The writer reiterates as if to insist that he is pleased (*eudokeō*), that he delights or takes pleasure not only in weakness (i.e., singular; cf. 1 Cor. 9:22) but also "weaknesses, insults, hardships, persecutions, and calamities." The limitation and frustration entangled with the experience of revelation, desire, and writing (especially the self) are neither removed nor circumvented. The

[69] Furnish, *II Corinthians*, 550.
[70] Brian Price, *A Theory of Regret* (Durham: Duke University Press, 2017), 139.

thorn persists. Instead, the writer rewrites himself as one vanquished and vanished. Power is neither restored nor alternatively achieved; it is undone. Once again taking recourse to a list, the writer, not unlike Barthes in the final pages of his autobiography,[71] resorts to matters that are mundane and routine in the context of his life.

Ultimately, the writer's self emerges in the very movements and gestures whereby it deflects and is deflected. Here, the forward-looking, active, intentional resolve of taking pleasure in the circumstantial and anecdotal is placed in tension with a backward-looking narrativization of past happenings. At the intersection of the two is a sort of withdrawal and acquiescence: the writer neither allows his self to be wholly checked and thwarted, nor is there any further aggression, no push toward, no ambition, no determination. The figure of Paul—Paul as Author, the myth of Paul—exists and functions the way it does because it is fueled by a self-reinforcing feedback loop: the Paul we imagine simultaneously precedes and exceeds the letters. Meanwhile, Paul the writing subject occupies—however fleetingly, transiently, ephemerally—a space between, an *atopia* wherein all I catch of the writer is a glimmer, a trace, perceived indirectly and peripherally in relation to his act of writing.

The customary reading wherein the Corinthians hold to a particular standard of social and spiritual status, they challenge Paul's status on those grounds, and Paul engages in a rhetorical strategy whereby he effectively says "I could but I will not because I am better than that, and I will show you why and to what extent by elevating the exact opposite to the stature of an ideal, and take pride, as it were, in my superior status on the basis of differently valued terms," does not reveal the person of Paul but rather ideologically inscribed and prescribed virtues of humility, service toward others, and an acceptance of one's plot in life. But the subversion is a chimera. Nothing has really changed. The terms remain the same, as well as an impulse toward boasting, superiority, a hierarchy, a valuation. It contributes to the fabrication of a "Paul" that is only a simulacrum that functions representatively and symbolically. What

---

[71] Barthes, *Roland Barthes*, 183–84. Labeled "Biography," these two pages list dates of what one might call various life events: the writer's birth, the death of his father, places and periods of employment, education, medical history, etc. The list concludes with a parenthetical statement: "A life: studies, diseases, appointments. And the rest? Encounters, friendships, loves, travels, readings, pleasures, fears, beliefs, satisfactions, indignations, distresses: in. word: repercussions? —In the text—but not in the work."

is necessary, if we are to "resurrect" the writer,[72] is to rewrite the writer and his writing, in part, by attending to instances and gestures where the writer pushes back against not primarily the terms of the argument into which he has been interpellated but rather the connotations of his own self, including those wrought by his own hand. We will find him, so to speak, in the rustling, the oscillation, between the two.

"The flesh" where the writer's thorn is lodged is a visceral substance. Even as a metaphor, he experiences and knows it in his body. But the subject is forced to take shape in language. The necessity (*dei*) that motivates his discourse evokes a certain tyranny of writing. For something to be described as necessary is to imagine it in terms of the imperative and Natural, the mandatory and inescapable. But writing also holds out the potential of the systems that govern it, that translate it into myth and Doxa. The very structure of this sentence (viz., 2 Cor. 12:1) reflects a desire to retreat from what is "necessary," from what "must be," even as he performs it. This mode of self-writing refracts what Pontalis called "the splendid and sinister marriage of language and death."[73] The writer juxtaposes necessity and the meaningless "must" to sufficiency (*arkeō*) and pleasure. Together they gesture toward a sense of equivalence and equilibrium, of continuance and satisfaction. Recalling what Barthes said of stupidity—namely, that it fascinated him, which he regarded as the feeling appropriate to the intractable—the writer's thorn, his weaknesses, become a language that provides the illusion of possession in order to elude being possessed.[74]

In Barthes's final book, *Camera Lucida*, "Photography becomes a project of 'resurrection,' related to refinding his mother, with all the pain, irony and suffering . . . involved in the (possible) invention of the photograph of his mother, which the book, apparently, does not allow us to see."[75] As Anderson explains:

> Barthes' quest for the meaning of photography leads him as if back to the beginning, to a photograph of his mother, which uniquely among his

---

[72] I'm speaking here in the sense of Michelet à la Barthes. See Roland Barthes, *Michelet*, trans. Richard Howard (Berkeley: University of California Press, 1992); Stafford, *Phenomenon and Myth*, 181–86; Michael Moriarty, *Roland Barthes* (Stanford: Stanford University Press, 1991), 187–88.
[73] Pontalis, *Love of Beginnings*, 13.
[74] See ibid., 34.
[75] Stafford, *Phenomenon and Myth*, 215.

photographs of her seems to reveal "the truth of the face that I loved." Strangely, however, this is not a photograph of his mother as he could have known her. It is not a photograph taken during their life together. Instead it is a picture of her, aged five, posing with her brother outside a Winter Garden.[76]

Like the writer of 2 Corinthians says of the unrepeatable revelations—which are twice removed, doubly sealed and protected, by virtue of the fact that the writer says he is speaking of someone else who experienced these things— Barthes writes:

> I cannot show you the Winter Garden Photo. It exists only for me. For you it would be nothing but an indifferent photo, one of a thousand manifestations of the "banal"; it cannot in any way constitute the visible object of a science; it cannot establish an objectivity, in the positive sense of the term; at most it might appeal to your studium: a period, clothes, photogenic subject matter; but in the photo, for you, there would be no wound.[77]

Knight argues that "if Barthes declines to reproduce the Winter Garden Photo, it cannot be for the reasons given in the bracketed apology that has so often been taken at face value."[78] She suggests that the Winter Garden Photograph is "simply an invention, a transposition of [a] 'real' photo to a setting that provides Barthes with the symbolism of light and revelation appropriate to a recognition scene and to his inversion of the *camera obscura* of photography into a *chambre claire*."[79] I am inclined to argue that the heavenly journey of 2 Corinthians 12 is similarly invented and that utterances heard cannot be repeated both because they do not exist as such and because they would fail to wound. It would be without a punctum, without a thorn.

It seems to me that, in the context of a letter, an autobiographical scene like the one we encounter in 2 Cor. 12:1-10 may come close to resembling a photograph. Ferguson writes that "the *journal intime* sometimes makes a certain, very relative, claim to being a 'pur signifiant', in that it is concerned with writing the inconsequential 'n'importe quoi' [anything at all] (as Gide puts it) of quotidian existence. Accordingly, its interests may lie more in the fact that

---

[76] Anderson, *Autobiography*, 73.
[77] Barthes, *Camera Lucida*, 73.
[78] Knight, *Barthes and Utopia*, 265.
[79] Ibid., 266.

it circumscribes a place of secrecy, than in the specific secrets it contains."[80] The self-narrations portraying matters of personal history we find in letters are very similar to *journaux intimes*. Together, they share in common with the photograph the same tense. Barthes writes: "Not only is the photograph never, in essence, a memory (whose grammatical expression would be the perfect tense, whereas the tense of the photograph is the aorist), but it actually blocks memory, quickly becomes a counter-memory."[81] The writer of 2 Corinthians says, regarding his self, only "I don't not know" and "that-has-been."[82]

---

[80] Ferguson, *Diaries Real and Fictional*, 27.
[81] Barthes, *Camera Lucida*, 91. See also Marcus, *Autobiography*, 102.
[82] See Barthes, *Camera Lucida*, 94, 100, and *passim*.

5

The Death of Paul

Letters are by nature a queer "dialogue": they are a "conversation," a "correspondence" with an absent Other.[1] David Fredrickson describes them as "illusory and insubstantial because the writer's presence and voice are creatures of the *recipient's* fantasy. It is less the skill of the writer and more the *pothos* of the recipient that turns a letter into an image. Longing is creative."[2] Commentary on letters, meanwhile, is a constrained and peculiar sort of voyeurism. Both genres reflect situations in which "language is born of absence."[3] In *A Lover's Discourse*, Barthes "stages" the subject (both speaker and topic) of the book's title in a way that, among other things, demonstrates through literary embodiment an inescapable and irreconcilable "exchange." Composed and structured in fragments—"figures" that mark the suspended and accidental "incidents" that manifest or confront free of narrative—the book neither unfolds nor plots the subject, but rather imitates its assemblage.[4] Reading the letters of Paul, a desire for the writer emerges in us: we want to know him. Paul is dead, in the literal sense, but he lives on figuratively, both as a text and as an operation of a text (his letters).[5] What lives on is no longer an historical person but a fabric of signifiers that paradoxically reads against

---

[1] "On the telephone the other is always in a situation of departure; . . .*I'm going to leave you,* the voice on the telephone says with each second" (Barthes, *Lover's Discourse*, 115; emphasis in original).

[2] David E. Fredrickson, *Eros and the Christ: Longing and Envy in Paul's Christology* (Minneapolis: Fortress Press, 2013), 18.

[3] Barthes, *Lover's Discourse*, 16.

[4] Ibid., 8: "To let it be understood that there was no question here of a love story (or the history of a love), to discourage the temptation of meaning, it was necessary to choose an *absolutely insignificant* order."

[5] "As an institution, the author is dead: his civil status, his biographical person have disappeared; disposed, they no longer exercise over his work the formidable paternity whose account literary history, teaching, a public opinion had the responsibility of establishing and renewing; but in the text, in a way, I *desire* the author: I need his figure (which is neither his representation nor his projection), as he needs mine (except to 'prattle')" (Barthes, *Pleasure*, 27; emphasis in original).

the historical self of the writer. They are apophatic words, and reading them positively is to fill in the otherwise fecund void, to complete a circuit.

The writing of one's self is always partial due to the exigencies of narrative selection, the limitations of perspective, and the impossibility of documenting one's own death in the (hi)story.[6] This chapter, therefore, considers two fragments from the letter to the Philippians: first, the writer's reflections on whether, given the circumstances of his imprisonment, death or life is more preferable (Phil. 1:19-26); and second, his curriculum vitae (Phil. 3:4b-6), which lists tokens of his identity and life that he discounts as filth. Both texts are etched with the trace of failure.[7] Philippians 1:12-26 reflects failure and an attempt to rise above it through acceptance: the writer is imprisoned but the message progresses undaunted. Inversely, Phil. 3:4b-8 reflects an ironic embrace of failure over success: though "blameless" with regard to so many things that once counted, the writer casts them off in pursuit of something that can only ever be imperfect and incomplete, or else be reached only in death. There seems to be a contradiction, however: in turning failure into success of whatever kind, in reimagining failure, we subvert failure and effectively erase it; we absorb and assimilate it into an ideology of success. But failure prior to being salvaged, before signification and determination (even if we grant that naming it failure implies a system), brushes up against so many familiar Barthesean tropes: stupidity, the novelistic, the Neutral—in a word, it is the fabric of the (writing) self. Here, in perhaps the most personal of Paul's letters, we may come closest to encountering what Barthes describes as "a horizontal discourse: no transcendence, no deliverance, no novel (though a great deal of the fictive)."[8]

Failure (1:12-26)

Indifference

The first figure encountered in the writer's self-narration of Phil. 1:12-20 is indifference. The segment is at once a report on the writer's situation and an appeal to readers to read that situation in a particular fashion. The writer

---

[6]   Marcus, *Autobiography*, 6, drawing on Paul de Man, "Autobiography as De-facement."
[7]   See Jay Twomey, "'Though We May Seem to Have Failed': Paul and Failure in Steve Ross' *Blinded*," in *Reading with Feeling: Affect Theory and the Bible*, ed. Fiona Black and Jennifer Koosed (Atlanta: Semeia Studies, forthcoming).
[8]   Barthes, *Lover's Discourse*, 7.

seems to say, in effect, that while his circumstances (viz., imprisonment) may appear one way (e.g., dire), they should be valued otherwise (e.g., fortunate). The writer points out that the things that would seem to confine and prohibit the ongoing dissemination of "the gospel" and the successful execution of his message have in fact assured both. Everyone responsible for securing his incarceration has come to know why he is there, and others have been emboldened to "speak the word . . . without fear," thereby carrying on the work. To be sure, in the writer's view, some of the latter are not acting from the best motives: proclaiming Christ "out of selfish ambition," seeking somehow to add to his grief. At this, the writer evinces a gesture of indifference: "What does it matter?" To which he answers, none. "Christ is proclaimed in every way."

As we have seen already in the treatments of the letters to the Romans and to the Corinthians, commentators attend closely to matters of form and function in their efforts to make sense of the material, reconstruct the author, and conform both to the myth of Paul.[9] In the process, interpreters stress rhetorical convention and the writer's comportment: the writer's narrative (re)presentation of himself conforms to convention and, more importantly, that conformity determines the *behavior* of the narrated self. It is not the actual behavior of the actual self but the *image-at-one's-disposal* behaving, acting, bearing properly in accordance with expectation, whether real or perceived, itself shaped and determined by the convention. Despite appearances, there is no "bare rehearsal of facts" in the narration but display, spectacle, and signification.[10]

---

[9] See, e.g., Ben Witherington, *Paul's Letter to the Philippians: A Socio-Rhetorical Commentary* (Grand Rapids: Eerdmans, 2011), 71–74. Witherington strives to make clear that this is a *narratio*, outlining what identifies it as such, explaining what would be expected in and of it, elaborating on the purposes of *narratio* as such, and even responding to those who have argued against this being viewed as a *narratio*. He notes that those who disagree do so on the grounds of content. In other words, it is not simply narrative, but *narratio*: a twice-functioning rhetorical device both at the level of "the original" and at the level of the contemporary commentary. "It was important . . . that the style of the *narratio* comport with the style and tone of what followed it, sending the right sort of signals, emotional and otherwise. *Rhet. ad Heren.* 1.13 stresses that since ethos and the personality of the speaker are at the fore here, the style must comport with the person and his personality and should make clear any change of fortune that the audience, which has a personal relationship with the speaker, needs to know about" (72). Paul A. Holloway (*Philippians* [Minneapolis: Fortress Press, 2017]) treats Philippians as a letter of consolation (1-10, 31-37). In keeping with that genre, Philippians offers "a series of *solacia*, or consolatory arguments" of which 1:12-26 provides three and 3:1ff is part of a fourth, and all have to do with "'the things that really matter' (1:10a)" (82). He says of 1:12-26 that ". . .Paul is offering a model for enduring hardship. . ." (85).

[10] According to Witherington, Cicero stressed that "the actions, language (style), and character of the orator should all be on display in the *narratio*, which should not be seen as a bare rehearsal of facts" (*Philippians*, 72).

The writer begins, "but I want you to know," which is to say that he inscribes a desire for the thinking that he understands or imagines his readers to possess to change, to be other than how it is. He seeks resonance over dissonance on the matter of his circumstances, his recent history, his self, his way of interpreting his recent history and present circumstances, which includes his absence from his readers. He seems to inscribe a desire to be *read* a certain way and to not be read at all. "But" (*de*) indicates that what the writer presents here is an alternative account that ultimately results in a different story, one narrated by a character within it, who consequently presumes to possess a unique and authoritative perspective on it. Indeed, he presumes to see things from a point of view that perfectly blends those of a primary participant in it and the writer of it, one inside the story and one presumably outside of it. It is as if the writer wants even to read himself and to be read by himself-qua-character, to open himself up to that character so as to be rewritten.

But with respect to the writer's self-narrative, we are not dealing with competing versions or renditions of something objectively present and prior. Rather, the things themselves—the writer's circumstances, the events precipitating them, the results of them, and so forth—are all subject to the discoursing of them, the storying of them. Bockmuehl describes the writer here as taking "great pains to relate his circumstances to the ministry of the gospel, formulating his own case as paradigmatic for the exhortation that follows in 1.27ff."[11] Taking great pains suggests that his way of seeing the matter was neither self-evident nor a foregone conclusion. More importantly, especially from a narrative perspective in which a defining characteristic of narrative discourse is the construction of causation, the writer's apparent concern to relate one thing (viz., his circumstances, "the things about me") to another (viz., "the gospel") reflects an effort to plot what might otherwise be perceived, at best, as a disparate cluster of random incidences, or, at worst, elements conscripted into an alternative plot that would be, from the writer's perspective, in unproductive tension with his own narrative. What is at stake, at least in part, is the writer's very self.

Just as will happen in Philippians 3, the writer contributes to the characterization of himself in the very act of characterizing the circumstances,

[11] Markus Bockmuehl, *The Epistle to the Philippians* (Peabody, MA: Hendrickson Publishers, 1998), 73.

the other characters in his narrative, and his relation to and attitude toward both. He, the writer, a character-narrator of a story both told only in retrospect and yet still unfolding, claims a special insight. He knows what is in an individual's heart and mind. Moreover, he is able, uniquely qualified even, to catalog groups of individuals according to fundamental essences he perceives them to share in common. Hence, the writer's image of himself is of one who is somehow distinct from both groups even despite his clear commonality with those in the group who preach from goodwill *toward him*.

But at the heart of it all is his question, "What does it matter?" All that matters is that Christ is proclaimed, the word is promulgated and published. In the writer's estimation, the success of that word proclaimed cannot be thwarted. Silence is the only thing that might threaten it, though even that holds out a hope and a promise for something that exceeds both the writer's presence and the verbal declaration. The letter itself, therefore, becomes an integral component of this shared and greater endeavor of the gospel, of the word and its dissemination. Moreover, it does so in a manner akin to Barthes's concern with returning to his own writing (viz., *Camera Lucida*) in the wake of mourning the death of his mother (as written in *Mourning Diary*).

But there is also a sense or trace of erasure here. The question—"What does it matter?"—is more indeterminate than it seems. While it no doubt refers to the motives of the groups in "preaching Christ," it could also be taken to refer to the writer's description thereof and to his involvement in this endeavor. His presence is of no consequence. Indeed, it is his absence from the readers that necessitates the letter in the first place, and that in turn is itself the dissemination and propagation of "the word," which is now pushed to the surface of the letter, alongside the writer's self, where it spreads into a field, a network, marked by plurality and irreducible difference. The writer's concern to focus attention on the word proclaimed regardless and, in the end, independently of the means of production blurs and obfuscates not only both of the groups he has been discussing but also himself. From within his position as a character-narrator, the writer attempts to remove himself from the equation that will ultimately add up to the readers' salvation, a salvation dependent upon loosening the self from the image-repertoire, upon absenting the self from an imposition or assertion of control, writing and unwriting the self. Indeed, by writing himself out of it, he evades and eliminates the emplotment of himself as a character in the narrative machinations of others competing for control of it.

Noting the "emotional quality of this discourse,"[12] Witherington focuses on the function of appealing to emotions or lending the narrative an emotional depth. Ultimately, this emotion is (or must be by Witherington himself) subordinated to the establishment of the writer's authority (i.e., so the readers will trust and respect him, listen to what he has to say, etc.) and incorporated into the model for imitation that he is supposedly positioning himself as. In other words, there neither is nor can be any direct emotional affect, let alone any subsequent knowledge infused with it and informed by it, stemming from the writer's raw, unqualified, unrefined reaction to either his incarceration or the behaviors of those outside (i.e., as he sees them and wants his readers to see them). It must, of necessity, be only an "emotional *quality*" employed in service to his rhetorical purposes. Yet, there is an ironic tension here insofar as scholars and ordinary readers alike still want to hear in these emotional longings something even more real and indicative of the writer's actual self. And if we are to find in both the writer and his letter a text rather than a work, and bliss rather than pleasure, it is fitting that we should do so. Hence, Barthes writes: "Emotion: why should it be antipathetic to bliss . . .? It is a disturbance, a bordering on collapse: something perverse, under respectable appearances; emotion is even, perhaps, the slyest of losses, for it contradicts the general rule that would assign bliss a fixed form: strong, violent, crude: something inevitably muscular, strained, phallic."

The relationship between mourning, memory, work, and writing in *Mourning Diary* (and in *Camera Lucida*) highlights the impenetrability and ineffability of the Other and vice versa. The mutual construction of each by one another and the subsequent responses to those constructions magnify the fact that we are already and always only ever in conversation with images and semblances. The writer's emotions are indeed a disturbance, and discomfort with them is reflected in Witherington's impulse to rein them in. But the writer himself, not only here but also elsewhere (recall, e.g., 2 Cor. 2:4; Phil. 3:18), is barely able to contain them.

This entire section is replete with signs and signifiers, and it is marked by a desire on the part of the writer to act politically, to effect a re-signification. The writer's chains, already a metonymy for imprisonment, for forced

---

[12] Witherington, *Philippians*, 73.

confinement,[13] function in the hands of commentators as something more closely resembling a symbol. For example, while Witherington accepts its plain sense meaning,[14] he goes on to suggest that it may mean "Paul is chained to Christ. Christ's treatment is replicated in Paul's treatment, and Christ's destiny is Paul's destiny."[15] Never minding that it is difficult to imagine who would see the writer's fetters as a clear sign of the reason for his imprisonment without being directed to read them that way, it may be better to consider the chains in relation to writing. Regardless of what they may be said to connote, the chains denote capture and confinement. They are the materialization of arrest. Analogously, the writer is bound by the text and to the text. He himself has become a text. And in the face of this, woven into the fabric of a text, this writer asks, "What does it matter?" The question signals withdrawal. It is a figure of the Neutral whereby the writer refuses to choose between in order to occupy an alternative space, a non-space, an *atopia*.

Indecency

Jane Gallop reflects on a question raised by Derrida in his essay on Lyotard in *The Work of Mourning*: "How to leave him alone without abandoning him?" One might wonder, in the face of 1:21-26, whether the writer ever pondered anything similar with respect to the Philippians. The writer certainly exhibits an ironic reticence, a hesitation, even a degree of ambivalence and unease that inevitably surfaces in the face of death and loss. The alternative—an inability or refusal to leave without abandoning—lies at the heart of "the myth of Paul" and of conscripting, appropriating, exploiting, and deploying "Paul" in ways that seem to be at odds with the very things he writes that so many are wont to understand and inhabit. Barthes notes that "'pleasure' . . . sometimes extends to bliss, sometimes is opposed to it,"[16] and the latter would appear to be the case in such readings.

---

[13] Witherington (*Philippians*, 79, n. 29) notes that "the description of Paul's condition and access to other Christians here in Philippians does not comport with the description of Roman prisons and their protocol as described in Wansink, *The Experience and Rhetoric of Paul's Imprisonments*" (cf. Tamez, "Philippians," 11–18).

[14] Witherington, *Philippians*, 79: "it is evident to others that Paul has been arrested and chained because of his Christian witness."

[15] Ibid., 79.

[16] Barthes, *Pleasure*, 19.

Gallop recognizes that this is a question of mourning but suggests that it is also "a question about the ethics of quotation."[17] She points to another place where Derrida identifies a "double law" that dictates "out of fidelity, one ought to quote [the dead, absent author] in the desire to let the other speak (again) but one should not, one should not be content to quote."[18] Gallop explains that this double law is about being content with limiting oneself to quoting without commentary, with circumscribing oneself in perfect faithfulness to the voice of the one quoted, while at the same time denying the contentment that would accompany quotation. She identifies the problem as one of both complacency and the question of containment because quoting entails selection: deciding where to start and stop, to cut off, the words of another and their rehearsal.

Derrida's statement continues, "I thus must quote but also interrupt the quotation,"[19] which recalls Barthes's remarks concerning the work of commentary referenced at the start of this book: "The work of commentary, once it is separated from any ideology of totality, consists precisely in *manhandling* the text, *interrupting* it."[20] Gallop asks: "If quoting without interruption seems, in a first moment, to be a way of avoiding indecency, is quoting *with* interruption a better way of avoiding indecency or is it instead an ethic of indecency?"[21] Drawing on what Derrida says in "The Deaths of Roland Barthes," she notes that there is ultimately a choice not between fidelity and infidelity but between two incompatible infidelities: "Either we quote and thus silence our own voice, or we speak without quoting and relegate the other to silence. What is lost in either case is the 'exchange,' the possibility of two voices speaking to each other. The ethics of quotation would seem to be an ethics of dialogue."[22]

It seems that the writer anticipates a very particular positive outcome to his situation in v. 19. If "deliverance" (*sōteria*) signifies his acquittal and release, things did not play out that way. In the face of that, commentators like Witherington[23] have to reimagine the writer's wish as an assertion of something else: God will provide some sort of spiritual fortitude, or a less

---

[17] Gallop, *Deaths of the Author*, 76.

[18] Ibid., 77, citing Jacques Derrida, *Mémoires pour Paul de Man* (Paris: Galilée, 1988), 64; Gallop's translation.

[19] Cited in Gallop, *Deaths of the Author*, 78.

[20] Barthes, *S/Z*, 15.

[21] Gallop, *Deaths of the Author*, 78–79, emphasis in original.

[22] Gallop, *Deaths of the Author*, 78–79.

[23] Witherington, *Philippians*, 83–84. See also his excursus on honor/shame language (87–89) where he primarily emphasizes something akin to what he does in his comments on Phil. 3, viz., Paul's

harrowing death, or vindication by virtue of the Gospel's unimpeded success, perhaps even energized and furthered by the writer's martyrdom.

Most commentators also see in the writer's pronouncement an echo of Job 13:16.[24] As Bockmuehl puts it: "Paul's assertion is in fact laced with an unmarked but highly evocative Old Testament quotation: in analogous circumstances of innocent affliction the righteous Job, too, says, 'Even this will turn out for my deliverance.'"[25] What interests me is the way this intertextual reference, whether it is an allusion on the part of the writer or a recognition on the part of a reader, activates and employs another story in order to flesh out the one presently being crafted and at work on the surface, and especially the troubling that manifests in these operations of quotation.

According to Bockmuehl, "Paul weaves into his discourse the words of a biblical man of faith which . . . would evoke in a biblically literate readership both the tense drama and the reassurance of a familiar text."[26] However, he rightly goes on to point out that "given the absence of OT quotations from Philippians and the likely background of Paul's original audience, it is not clear to what extent the apostle could have expected his readers to understand such specific allusions."[27] Hence, he concludes (it seems somewhat grudgingly, if not desperately), "in any case the fact of Paul's own intimate knowledge of the Septuagint makes such 'intertextual' echoes of Scripture an important clue to the structures and formation of his own thought."[28]

Perhaps Bockmuehl is right. Perhaps the writer's evocation of Hebrew scripture, regardless of the degree it resonates with his imagined readers,

---

reversal of cultural norms, transforming apparently shameful things into honorable things, or, in this case, urging his readers to see it that way.

[24] See, e.g., Bockmuehl, *Philippians*, 82–83; Gordon D. Fee, *Paul's Letter to the Philippians* (Grand Rapids: Eerdmans, 1995), 130; John Reumann, *Philippians* (New Haven: Yale University Press, 2008), 210, 232–33, 243; Tamez, "Philippians," 60; Stephen Fowl, "The Use of Scripture in Philippians," in *Paul and Scripture: Extending the Conversation*, 163–84, ed. Christopher D. Stanley [Atlanta: Society of Biblical Literature, 2012]). There are no direct quotes from the Hebrew Bible in Philippians, and what few allusions or echoes (more subtle than allusion, according to Reumann) there *may* be are vague and indirect (see, for example, 2:10 [Isa. 45:23]; 2:15-16 [Deut. 32:5; Dan. 12:3; Isa. 49:4; 65:23]; 4:3 [Exod. 32:32, 33; Ps. 69:28; Dan. 12:1]; 4:5 and 7 [Isa. 26:3]). To wit, it could be argued that these are as much the product of any given reader's intertexts and desire to see something other than and beyond the letter itself as they are something planted by the author's design.

[25] Bockmuehl, *Philippians*, 82.

[26] Ibid.

[27] Ibid. Cf. Fowl, "Scripture in Philippians," 171: "Although the amount of textual material here is not large, Job 13:16 and Phil 1:19 are the only places where this precise form of words occurs in Scripture." Fowl suggests that the lack of introduction results in the allusion adding something to the reading experience of those in the know without detracting anything from those who are unfamiliar.

[28] Bockmuehl, *Philippians*, 83.

sheds light on his self-understanding and his perception of his circumstances, the world around him, his readers, and so forth. Any narrative evoked, even if unintentionally, plays a fundamental role in determining, mediating, and characterizing all of the figures in play, resulting in an entanglement wherein whatever we purport to find, to somehow understand, and to claim, exists in and as an instance of intersection, a multistoried story irrevocably ensconced in layers of narrative in infinite regress. The echo perhaps offers the writer the reassurance of a *completed* narrative (viz., the Book of Job) vis-à-vis one yet to be written (viz., the outcome of the writer's imprisonment and trial, and even of the letter and the Philippians' response). Suggesting one narrative as a means of reading another narrative certainly provides contemporary commentators with as much insofar as it offers the security of a source and foundation; it establishes an Author and a work.

In *The Pleasure of the Text*, Barthes suggests that the writer takes a certain perverse or indecent pleasure in "the form of a drift."[29] Such drifting occurs, Barthes explains, "whenever *I do not respect the whole* . . . whenever social language, the sociolect, *fails me*."[30] Consequently, he labels such drifting "*the Intractable*—perhaps even: Stupidity."[31] I see in the echo of Job a drifting on the part of the writer, a perverse and indecent pleasure that signals a text of bliss by virtue of "quotation without quotation marks."[32] Barthes describes this as one means by which the text of bliss is able to thwart and exceed language from within. The writer of Philippians gestures toward the text of bliss: he does not cite Job; he drifts with what comes to him.[33] However, the impulse on the part of commentators is to contain the excessiveness, to make Philippians at best a text of pleasure, rendered as a work and made readerly through citation.

I perceive a certain indecency in the evocation of the character, story, and words of Job, but in such a way as to leave him alone without abandoning him. What better way is there for the writer to absent himself than for him to imagine himself, already a character in the narration of his own self, as yet

---

[29] Barthes, *Pleasure*, 18.
[30] Ibid., 18 and 19; emphasis in original.
[31] Ibid., 19; emphasis in original.
[32] Ibid., 32.
[33] Ibid., 36: "Proust is what comes to me, not what I summon up; not an 'authority,' simply a *circular memory*. Which is what the inter-text is: the impossibility of living outside the infinite text—whether this text be Proust or the daily newspaper or the television screen: the book creates the meaning, the meaning creates life" (emphasis in original).

another character, and one that likely would have been lost on non-Jewish readers and is presumably still lost on any number of readers today? There emerges a text of bliss, a neutral, writerly text. Even as additional layers of perversion and indecency unfold in the proliferation of readings and threaten to make the writer and the letter texts of pleasure, readerly works, the writer both eludes and persists.

The writer's "earnest expectation and hope" that by speaking freely, unrestrainedly, Christ will be exalted in *his body* (v. 20) signals a return of the figure, as well as a return to the specific space the writer then occupies. But what is the speaking and the body of a writer? "Paul" is a man of letters, and the letter itself is not speech but writing. Moreover, time irreparably complicates matters. The writer here, at the time of writing, in the narration of himself, is quasi-foreshadowing a longed for and anticipated ending that both is and is not (yet) written. Thus, the speaking body of the writer is the corpus.

Indecision

The writer's reference to dying as "gain" signals a sense of desire for release. In an undated fragment of Barthes's *Mourning Diary*, he writes:

> *Suicide*
>
> How would I know I don't suffer any more, if I'm dead?
>
> In the imagination I might have of my death (which everyone has), I added to the anguish of disappearing soon the equal anguish of the *unendurable* pain I would cause her.[34]

Regarding the possibility that the writer is contemplating suicide, Witherington forcefully declares: "I completely disagree with [the] assertion that a Jew like Paul might be considering suicide here. That would fly in the face of not only his heritage but also what he says here at the end of the narratio."[35] He goes on to clarify that "what Paul says here is nothing like other utterances about

---

[34] Barthes, *Mourning Diary*, 247; emphasis in original.
[35] Witherington, *Philippians*, 89, n. 71. Withering references J. A. Droge and J. D. Tabor, *A Noble Death* (San Francisco: HarperCollins, 1992), 121; S. E. Fowl, *Philippians* (Grand Rapids: Eerdmans, 2005), 55–59; and the critique of the suicide proposal by N. Clayton Croy, "'To Die Is Gain' (Philippians 1:19-26): Does Paul Contemplate Suicide?" *JBL* 122 (2003): 517–31. He goes on to explain that the phrase "death is gain" was not understood by Paul "as an escape plan or as a relief from a terrible or burdensome or chronically ill life, but as a means to draw closer to Christ" (90).

death being gain because life is hateful, horrible, burdensome, or disease-ridden. Paul does not view his life as Greek tragedy and has no death wish or lust for martyrdom."[36] Hence, the writer's apparent indecision is nothing more than "feigned perplexity" (*diaporesis*).[37] Bockmuehl[38] effectively imagines the self-reflective soliloquy as an aside, which suggests that the narrative is somehow responsible for determining both its narrator and itself, as it were, dictating its continuance.[39] If the issue is that the writer is betraying concern about the outcome of his impending trial and uncertainty over whether he will be released from prison, and the intent is to portray himself as feeling a particular way in response to that anxiety, then the choice he makes is not one of living or dying in any real sense so much as it is attitudinal, metaphorical, ideational. Minimizing the material reality of the writer's chains and reducing the writer's position and deliberation to nothing more than a positive outlook are dangerous maneuvers in that they risk spiritualizing the harsh reality of confinement and suffering. If the writer's indecision is only feigned, then it is not him that we encounter but only a disingenuous subterfuge and an unseemly simulacrum. It would be better to recognize that the writer is caught between two strong desires, one personal and one seemingly more focused on those to whom he is writing, and to see that the space of disjuncture is precipitated by the fact that he has no control over his circumstances; he has no real say in the matter of his imprisonment and release nor in the terms of his reception. The only recourse he has available in order to influence the outcome in such a way as to both depart and to remain is to write, withdraw, and be silent at trial. But here, in the text, the writer forever oscillates in the figure of desire.

Marked by numerous fissures—life and death, Christ and gain, departure and lingering, desire and necessity, himself and those to whom he is writing,

[36] Witherington, *Philippians*, 90, n. 76, referencing Euripides, Sophocles, Plato, Libanius, and Josephus.

[37] Ibid., 90; referencing Croy, "'To Die Is Gain,'" 525–31. According to Croy, it amplifies the impact of the concluding "decision," and it was a commonplace mode of expression. "Quintilian, for example, says that this sort of figure of thought lends the impression of truth and sincerity to one's reflections as one shows one's humanity (*Inst. Or.* 9.2.19; Witherington, *Philippians*, 90).

[38] "Although it was not Paul's primary purpose, the discussion of [1:18b-20] has introduced the earnest question of his attitude in the face of death" (Bockmuehl, *Philippians*, 87).

[39] Barthes, *S/Z*, 178: "If we have a realistic view of *character*, if we believe that [in this case, Paul] has a life off the page, we will look for motives for this interruption. If we have a realistic view of *discourse*, if we consider the story being told as a mechanism which must function until the end, we will say that since the law of narrative decrees that it continue, it was necessary that the word [in this case, suicide] not be spoken. . . . *The character and the discourse are each other's accomplices* (emphases in original).

escape and work—the writer's remark about being caught between the two, and his reference to desire, refracts a glimmer of the Neutral. The writer is doubly split: internally and externally. Here, he describes himself as conflicted within, torn between a desire for himself and a concern for, or a sense of responsibility toward, his audience. But he is also split by virtue of his position as a character-narrator. The writer's body, confined to a prison cell, immobilized by shackles, subjected to a trial, facing the concrete possibility of being sentenced to death and subsequently killed, is regarded by the writer as an instrument of mission, and as a palimpsest on which has been written and rewritten the story of Christ's own suffering. The writer is not seeking to separate himself from the body, to escape the physical as if it were a mere husk transporting his true inner self from place to place. The writer's body and his writing, his *body of work* are inseparable. The exaltation of Christ in his body is, thus, both integrated with, and independent of, a future yet to be written for the writer, though also already history for us. In the end, the writer writes as if to say, with Barthes, "I live without any concern for posterity, no desire to be read later on . . ., complete acceptance of vanishing utterly, no desire for a 'monument.'"[40]

Filth (3:1-14)

Readers customarily regard the writer's autobiographical statements in Phil. 3:4b-6 as historical details denoting concrete realities of Paul's actual life. To wit, these statements have long functioned as a cornerstone upon which so many historical reconstructions have been built in various biographies of Paul, signaling his life story and providing the basis for so many subsequent stories of that story. Moreover, they also function as the point of departure for the writer's argument as it is traditionally read: namely, the writer's heritage and past practice in the traditions associated with that heritage once counted for something, but now they no longer do so on account of the surpassing value of knowing Christ, which devalues or renders effectively valueless and irrelevant

[40] Barthes, *Mourning Diary*, 234. Cf. "You yourselves are our letter, written on our hearts, to be known and read by all; and you show that you are a letter of Christ, prepared by us, written not with ink but with the Spirit of the living God, not on tablets of stone but on tablets of human hearts" (2 Cor. 3:2-3).

everything else by comparison. For both the historical reconstruction and the argument, it is presumed that behind these words is an author, especially if one means by that term "someone who claims the authority to write one's life and whose 'mind' is constructed beyond the texts in which his or her 'I' is inscribed."[41] It is believed that these words in some way reflect nothing less than Paul's actual self, the real Paul, here represented and presented *by his own hand*. Bockmuehl describes these verses as "a remarkably forthright testimony about his pre-Christian past, which in this form is unmatched anywhere else in his writings."[42] The thrust of both the passage and the standard interpretations of it are straightforward. Thus, he states:

> Paul sets out . . . to use his own example in refuting the Judaizing position with its concomitant promises of enhanced religious and (at least implicitly) social prestige. To do so, he lists the impeccable Jewish pedigree by which he himself once set store, at a time when he adhered to a nationalistic position with great fervour and dedication. This personal example will serve as the negative backdrop against which to formulate his positive affirmation of faith in Christ.[43]

The self-narratives are first and foremost paraenetic.[44] The writer's self is not so much constructed and masked as it is merely (re)presented—simply shaped, colored, crafted, repackaged—in a manner that highlights matters and markers of the self to be discounted, whereby Paul positions himself as an

---

41 Melanie Johnson-DeBaufre, "Narrative, Multiplicity, and the Letters of Paul," in *The Oxford Handbook of Biblical Narrative*, 362–75, ed. Danna Nolan Fewell (Oxford: Oxford University Press, 2016), 365. Cf. Michel Foucault, "What Is an Author?", in *The Foucault Reader*, 101–20; ed. Paul Rabinow (1979; New York: Pantheon Books, 1984).

42 Bockmuehl, *Philippians*, 195.

43 Ibid., 194–95.

44 "As Craddock says, this appeal (including the autobiographical data) just like the Christ-hymn appeal has a paraenetic function—to produce mimesis, imitation" (Witherington, *Philippians*, 183; citing F. Craddock, *Philippians* [Atlanta: John Knox, 1985], 53). Elsewhere, Witherington argues that Paul uses himself (or appears to do so) as an example throughout Philippians. In 1:12-26 and in 3:1–4:1, he does so by of *synkrisis*, or comparison: in the former, the writer is providing the readers "with an example of how to behave in the face of adversities and possible adversaries" (Witherington, *Philippians*, 71; note also the excursus on "imitation" as "the highest form of education," 76–78). The language evokes a sense of mass (re)production. Barthes imagined humanity "doomed to Analogy, i.e., in the long run, to Nature," which writers strive to escape by means of "two contrary excesses, or call them two *ironies* which flout Analogy, either by feigning a spectacularly *flat* respect (this is the Copy, which is rescued), or by *regularly*—according to the regulations—distorting the imitated object (this is Anamorphosis)." He goes on to say, "when I resist analogy, it is actually the imaginary I am resisting: which is to say: the coalescence of the sign, the similitude of signifier and signified" (*Roland Barthes*, 44; emphasis in original).

example of one who thinks, lives, and acts in accordance with an alternative economy of significance.

Once these items are read as a profile and synopsis of Paul's former life, commentators naturally are obliged, both by their reading and by the constraints and expectations of the commentary genre, to unpack the meaning of the individual components, which is to say that they supplement and ultimately supplant the list with a narrative. So, for example, commentators begin with distinguishing between "four items in the inheritance of any Jewish male,"[45] only one of which is particular to the writer (viz., his tribe), and three specific and notable areas of accomplishment, which Malina and Neyrey refer to as his "manner of life."[46] Then, each item is glossed individually so that the series of statements function as a schema, an outline in which each item properly relates to those around it, providing a narrative, signifying a history, and connoting the real. Moreover, they combine for a cumulative effect that exceeds the sum of the parts.[47]

Admittedly, some commentators will caution that "the items cited are carefully selected to fit the present controversial setting, and must not be assumed to offer straightforward information about either Paul's life or his views before becoming a Christian,"[48] and some note that the "I" serves "both polemical and paradigmatic" functions.[49] I agree that the writer is not writing

---

[45] Reumann, *Philippians*, 512.

[46] Cited in Reumann, *Philippians*, 513. It is interesting to note that "circumcision" is a matter of both body and law, and "*genos*" is a matter of blood and ethnicity—the body expresses nothing, but it is a site of writing and of meaning. Witherington (*Philippians*, 198) thinks "Hebrew of Hebrews" is an issue of language: "It probably means a person who speaks Hebrew and came from a family where it was spoken . . . as opposed to a Diaspora Jew who never learned to speak it." From this he extrapolates: "This likely tells us something about Paul's upbringing and education, not merely in Tarsus that place of his birth but, as Acts 22 suggests, in Jerusalem" (198). "Tribe of Benjamin" associates Paul with his namesake, Saul, the first king of Israel, "most illustrious member of that tribe," the tribe's reputation of faithfulness toward Judah, its having been named after the only one of Jacob's twelve sons to have been born in the Promised Land (198). Ultimately, however, according to Witherington, the effect is cumulative: The preceding items "signify" "what [Paul] innately is by birth and upbringing" and the three that follow concern "what he once was and did, including his religious praxis" (199).

[47] ". . . Paul could claim all the best there is to claim about being a Jew, both religiously and ethnically" (Witherington, *Philippians*, 199).

[48] Bockmuehl, *Philippians*, 195; cf. Witherington, *Philippians*, 75: referring to Phil. 1:12-26, he asserts that "Paul's recounting of his circumstances and how they will likely turn out is not given for its own sake."

[49] Reumann, *Philippians*, 505. It is striking to me how illustrative are the remarks even of Darrell J. Dougherty, who is arguing from a deeply entrenched historical-critical perspective and yet still contends that "the portrait of the apostle and the understanding of Christian existence for which he serves as an example are deutero-Pauline. The concrete controversies that characterized Paul's own life are no longer in view. The teachings of Paul have been universalized. What we have here

autobiographically in order to know himself, express himself, or to reflect on the self as such, etc. Witherington states: "Paul is not defending his apostleship here or discoursing on his own background because he is in a sentimental mood. No, he is telling his own story in a mode that is modeled on Christ's story."[50]

Such caveats betray both an awareness of and a resistance to the curated and fragmentary nature of the self. However, while this might lead us to consider the inaccessibility of any "real" or "essential" Paul, these contingencies seem instead to serve the interest of signifying a "Paul" that is too big, too irreducible, too singular and unique. In a word, it serves to reify Paul and the ideas attributed to him in service to the dominant myth of Paul. "Despite the impressive catalog of his particular, fixed ethnic credentials that follow (3:5-6), Paul also is able to claim that he counts them and 'all things' as loss or 'dung' (3:7-8). Granted, Paul still 'has' these qualities (fixed identity), but he can give them up to gain something else (3:7-11) (his fluid identity)."[51] In the end, the self-narrative is perceived as an expression of the self, merely a conduit for conveying simultaneously the author's ideas and our ideas of the author (viz., humility, reevaluation, subservience to and in perpetual passionate pursuit of Christ), which are now in lockstep. Paul, the author, meets his opponents on their own terms in order to best them at their own game, and then to supersede that language by relativizing and minimizing its value—all without losing his self, even as he seems to ironically or paradoxically, and most of all intentionally, do just that: abandon the self for the sake of gaining and knowing Christ. That, in turn, is the thing to be imitated—less the idea or disposition itself than the manner of its manifestation, that is, not simply to abandon all else and yearn for Christ above all else, but to do so *like Paul*, the man we presume to know in and through and by this self-narration. All of this plays right into the operation of the myth because "the contradiction of ethnic/communal identity

---

represents the testimony of the apostle for believers in all times and places. From this perspective, the polemical teachings in Phil 3 have little to do with specific opponents. They apply rather to 'opponents' of every kind, wherever they appear. They reflect the self-understanding the faithful community, characterized by a fundamental dichotomy between the community and the outside world as such": ("Citizens of Heaven. Philippians 3:2-21 as a Deutero-Pauline Passage," *NTS* 41 [1995]: 102–22).

[50] Witherington, *Philippians*, 182.

[51] Joseph A. Marchal, *The Politics of Heaven: Women, Gender, and Empire in the Study of Paul* (Minneapolis: Fortress Press, 2008), 76.

as both fixed and fluid is not a sign of the argument's fracture and failure, but its adaptive efficacy."[52]

Typically, Phil. 3:4b-6 is read as a reference to the writer's past life with its privileges and achievements stated in order to indicate what trusting in the flesh means, which in turn, plays into the overarching thrust of the argument in this section, and again positions Paul as a model to be imitated.[53] Even though these things would have struck Greco-Roman readers in Philippi as odd, unsavory, or meaningless, they are still things *he* thinks may have once been boast-worthy at a particular time, among particular people, from a particular perspective.[54] Overlooking the complex and dynamic relationship and interplay between past and present in Philippians and in all self-narration (particularly in letters), commentators link "past" and "loss" thereby entangling point of view and focalization. Hence, in his concern to stress that "blameless" does not equate to either "faultless" or "perfect," Witherington states, as if the issue were obvious: "Paul is speaking here about his Pharisaic past, and perhaps speaking as he did as a Pharisee. . . . A text like 1 Cor. 15.9 makes perfectly clear that Paul the Christian knows in retrospect that Saul the Pharisee was certainly not without fault in God's eyes."[55] The "flesh" of which our writer is so fond, and to which readers themselves are naturally drawn, so rarely seems to possess its neutral sense of human skin and sinew. Even in popular parlance it takes on connotations of mortal conditionality or the body. But that in turn is followed by a second-order code whereby "more often than not, Paul uses this term in a loaded sense . . . a clearly moral sense," that is, referring to "fallen or wicked inclinations or desires resident in the mortal body."[56]

Hence, the construction of the self is a reactionary, oppositional, apophatic endeavor. But what so many commentators note about the writer's treatment of the opponents—namely, that the image of them is formed by epithets such that they become caricatures, less described than insulted[57]—might also

[52] Marchal, *The Politics of Heaven*, 77.
[53] See, e.g., Peter T. O'Brien, *The Epistle to the Philippians* (Grand Rapids: Eerdmans, 1991), 345–46; cf. Witherington, *Philippians*, 196 and 182.
[54] "In vv. 4-6 Paul lists those traits he could well have boasted about, if he were to evaluate them from a human and Jewish point of view" (Witherington, *Philippians*, 197–98).
[55] Witherington, *Philippians*, 200.
[56] Ibid., 196.
[57] Epithets equate to caricaturization if not characterization. Reumann (*Philippians*, 471, quoting Helmut Koester, "The Purpose of the Polemic of a Pauline Fragment (Philippians iii)." *NTS* 8 [1961–62]: 321) explains that Paul's aim "is not to describe the opponents, but to insult them" (cf. O'Brien, *Philippians*, 354, n. 48). For example, the writer's wordplay (e.g., incision versus circumcision), according to

be applicable to the writer as well. At issue is substance versus appearance, surface, *relation to*. The disgust conjured up by the writer's characterization of the so-called "dogs" signals aversion, utter contempt, repugnance, at the heart of which is a fundamental resistance to fundamental(ist) designations, classifications, categorizations, identifications. Hence, to doggedly ascribe, in turn, such things to the writer in our efforts to (re)construct "Paul" is to oppose the writer himself in the very effort to identify him and to write any biography of him. In other words, in the attempt to circumscribe an Author, to life-write "Paul," critics are inevitably forced to construct, appeal to, and adopt categories and classifications that differ in designation but are fundamentally the same *in kind*, overlooking or altogether ignoring the writer they want so desperately to hear. But it is the disgust itself that leaves a trace of the writer's self: his disdain for anything that would limit, conscript, or otherwise locate meaning or identity with something external, anything that would identify the self with, make the self identical to, something produced after the fact (i.e., a sociocultural identity), and to the connotations thereof being retroactively *applied to* the self, reducing it to something containable, capable of being pigeonholed, pinned in, pinned down.

At the heart of so many readings of either the Author behind or the writer within Philippians and other letters associated with "Paul" is an exegesis of the self as a text.[58] But there is an important difference between the two that is marked by the inadvertent but not insignificant or insubstantial shift from exegeting a work (Philippians—though also a text in its own right) to exegeting a text (the writer).

The comparison and contrast made in and by 3:4b-6 is not, according to most modern commentators, between Judaism and Christianity but rather between something like intrinsic value versus relative value: there is nothing innately bad or worthless about Judaism and Paul's observance thereof, but the value of knowing Christ trumps the writer's previous economy of

Reumann (*Philippians*, 467), disparages and inverts the opponents' language with the aim of making them laughable. The drive toward precise identification of the opponents is ironic insofar as it seems to reflect another resistance to the actual writer who, as with the revelations of 2 Cor. 12, refuses to name the opponents or to describe them more accurately, opting instead for caricatures and connotations. For an extended study of the opponents in Philippians that attempts to definitively identify them while also analyzing the writer's rhetoric vis-à-vis his own process of social identity formation, see Nikki, *Opponents and Identity in Philippians*; cf. idem., "Flexible Apostle," 88–96.

[58] Reumann (*Philippians*, 470) speaks to the character of the writer's response: "[his] defense will be personal, rather than exegetical."

significance.[59] Note, however, it is not Judaism but the signifiers of Judaism that are in play here, and identity (perhaps particularly vis-à-vis knowledge) is the theme. Typical of the so-called "New Perspective" approach, commentators dutifully explain that "Paul's problem was not that he couldn't make the grade; it was that he did make it, only to find out that it was the wrong standard of measurement."[60] Hence, the issue is not guilt so much as regret.[61]

Issues pertaining to and entangled with the so-called New Perspective on Paul form the backdrop to so much of the rhetorical work being performed among commentators interpreting these statements concerning the writer's supposed past. Debates where the New Perspective arises are debates about identity, the origins and sources of Paul's thought,[62] and Paul's attitudes toward Judaism vis-à-vis our own.

What is so curious to me, however, is not merely the preference for the discounted excellence of the imagined Paul depicted in Philippians 3 over the inescapable struggle of an imagined Paul in Romans 7 but what amounts to either an insistence on, or a taken-for-grantedness of, the former being more accurate, more true, more authentic of the "real" Paul. *Both* simultaneously support and stem from an image-repertoire. For me, "Paul" is not to be found in either Philippians 3 or Romans 7; rather, the writer is located in the contradiction between the two. Barthes describes "the blurring of contradictions" as "the bastard form of mass culture."[63] Better still, he states: "This is why, when we speak today of a divided subject, it is never to acknowledge his simple contradictions, his double postulations, etc.; it is a *diffraction* which is intended, a dispersion of energy in which there remains neither a central core nor a structure of meaning: I am not contradictory, I am dispersed."[64]

Recalling what Witherington said concerning Paul's mental outlook in Romans 7, why is it that Philippians is a check against Romans instead of the reverse? The answer is that our concern—understandably and, in many cases,

---

[59] Witherington (*Philippians*, 195) uses the term "transvalue" to describe the situation.

[60] Dean Flemming, *Philippians: A Commentary in the Wesleyan Tradition* (Kansas City: Beacon Hill Press, 2009), 165; cited in Witherington, *Philippians*, 201.

[61] See again Price, *Theory of Regret*; Twomey, "Though We May Seem to Have Failed."

[62] Seyoon Kim, *Paul and the New Perspective: Second Thoughts on the Origin of Paul's Gospel* (Grand Rapids: Eerdmans, 2001).

[63] Barthes, *Pleasure*, 41–42.

[64] Barthes, *Roland Barthes*, 143; emphasis in original.

rightly—has not been with the aesthetics, much less the erotics of the text (be it the writer or the writing), but with the myth of "Paul" and its operations. My point is not to argue against the New Perspective, per se; it is rather that the use of the letters, and the underlying conceptualization of them—that is, what they are perceived to be vis-à-vis the writer precedes and subsequently dictates the writing-self we distill from them and use to anchor them. Recalling again the quote from Marchal concerning the "adaptive efficacy" of the writer's arguments, perhaps Philippians 3 is nothing more than another prime example of what the writer professes in 1 Corinthians 9.

Matlock, drawing on Daniel Boyarin, concludes that "true Jewishness" for Paul ultimately has nothing to do with familial associations, shared cultural history, or maintaining prescribed socioreligious practices, but "paradoxically consists of participating in a universalism, an allegory that dissolves those essences and meanings entirely."[65] Arguably, then, the New Perspective betrays our own fear of failure. But were we to reconsider the possibility of Paul's failure, we might opt to regard it as a kind of utopian and heroic, if not antiheroic, maneuver that rejects mastery of its associations.[66] Drawing on Sara Ahmed, Jay Twomey notes that "those who fail to adhere to a norm are unhappy . . . because they cause unhappiness in others." This resonates with what the reader encounters both in Romans 7 (viz., the performance of internal conflict and turmoil) and in Philippians 1 (viz., the writer's "decision" to remain for the sake of the letter's recipients). Therefore, "in contrast [to] narratives setting Paul in opposition to failure, or treating Pauline failure as a path to success, or at least to a better life—Paul himself can also be imagined productively both as a sign of normative aspirations and as a character in need of a different trajectory thanks to those punishing norms; he both pursues and represents 'negating rhythms of self-continuity' and is himself a kind of affective impasse."[67]

---

[65] Matlock, "Almost Cultural Studies?," 454; citing Daniel Boyarin, *A Radical Jew: Paul and the Politics of Identity* (Berkeley: University of California Press, 1994), 94–95. See again Bird, *An Anomalous Jew*, 5–8.

[66] Twomey, "Though We May Seem to Have Failed," n.p., quoting Judith Halberstam, *The Queer Art of Failure* (Durham: Duke University Press, 2011), 11–12. He later notes, "For Halberstam, 'failure is what allows us to escape the punishing norms that discipline behavior and manage human development with the goal of delivering us from unruly childhoods to orderly and predictable adulthoods. Failure preserves some of the wondrous anarchy of childhood and disturbs the supposedly clean boundaries between adults and children, winners and losers.'"

[67] Twomey, "Though We May Seem to Have Failed," n.p., quoting Lauren Berlant, *Cruel Optimism* (Durham: Duke University Press, 2011), 113.

Twomey ultimately turns his attention to the trope of childhood and 1 Cor. 13:11 where the writer speaks of having once spoken, thought, and reasoned as a child. Childhood tends to be the stuff of nostalgia and sentimentality, a romanticized image conceivable only in retrospect and a trope that serves the myth of innocence. Barthes himself writes: "It is at this point of contact between the writing and the work that the hard truth appears to me: *I am no longer a child*." But then he asks: "Or else, is it the *ascesis* of pleasure which I am discovering?"[68] This seems to capture precisely Twomey's point when he notes that "at the same time . . . the heavy-handed, clichéd affirmation of childhood as a time of limitless possibility is itself a highly defensive controlling mechanism of its own."[69]

Twomey finds in the conclusion of Steve Ross's graphic novel *Blinded* a "Paul without Paul, or Saul for that matter," and suggests that "accepting the failure at the heart of Paul's project seems *not* to lead into a successful detour from or renewal of that project, but to its undoing."[70] It seems to me that this is exactly what Barthes envisions in regard to the dichotomy of success and failure. He writes: "A third category is possible: neither success nor failure: disgrace: marked, branded with the imaginary."[71]

The commonplace reading of Phil. 3:4b-6 is curious (if not altogether problematic) foremost because, as an instance of self-narration, it necessarily entails a complex dynamic wherein a writer writes about himself as an Other, and thus becomes a character-narrator in the process. Because they involve embedded focalization—one character's perspective is voiced within another character's perspective—character narrations are at best ambiguous and at worst unreliable. It is impossible to determine with any certainty who speaks, or who is responsible for the vision controlling the (re)presentation. Hence, it comes as no surprise that commentators debate whether the writer is speaking here about these particular things from the perspective of his former life or from the perspective he professes at the time of writing.

More than that, however, the relationship of these statements to the larger narrative unit is peculiar to me. They seem almost to float, as it were. The

---

[68] Barthes, *Roland Barthes*, 137; emphasis in original.
[69] Twomey, "Though We May Seem to Have Failed," n.p.
[70] Ibid.
[71] Barthes, *Roland Barthes*, 156. It is worth pointing out that Barthes arrives at this by way of "rereading himself" and "[discerning] in the very texture of each piece of writing a singular cleavage: that of *success/failure*" (emphasis in original).

items mentioned hang together as a list, a catalog, a canon of sorts—that is, by virtue of both its function (authoring and authorizing, constructing identity) and its form—that is not altogether unlike what we find in 2 Cor. 11:23-28. They function as a series of signifiers and relationships from the writer's image-repertoire—that persistent repository of images available to and thrust upon the writer, mediating his experience, which "is precisely defined by its coalescence (its adhesiveness), or again: its power of association"[72]— that both expose and produce a certain reality, or a certain likeness of the writer's self. Both in the form of their presentation and precisely because of the worthlessness and irrelevance retroactively ascribed to them, they do not constitute the writer's self or his past substantively, but rather refract only a sense that "this happened"; "this at once is and was." Despite the fact that he is writing to a thoroughly non-Jewish audience, no explanation or elaboration accompanies the terms. They are presented as if they speak for themselves, but to whom do they speak, and how? The are reality effects that resist the attribution of meaning.

If Phil. 3:4b-6 presents or functions as a reality effect, then two questions follow: first, what are scholars doing when they read these verses otherwise, or what are the consequences of reading these verses otherwise? And second, what is the writer doing in speaking this way, or what might be happening at the level of the writing? In other words, how might we read these statements in a way that takes seriously the atypical, non-narrative form of this "history," which seems to signal or function in a different manner than would a more conventional narrative?

Melanie Johnson-DeBaufre describes Paul as a man of story in two ways: "First, Paul is a central, even paradigmatic, character in both popular and scholarly versions of Christian origins, creating the illusion that there is a singular, coherent story of Paul that can be reconstructed from the seven letters widely accepted as Pauline, the six additional letters attributed to him, and the canonical and apocryphal acts in which Paul is a primary character."[73] The second way that Paul is a man of story is a bit more complex. Here it is not so much Paul as a character but Paul as a mind, a mind fundamentally shaped by an underlying narrative structure that informs his perception of

---

[72] Barthes, *Lover's Discourse*, 51.
[73] Johnson-DeBaufre, "Narrative, Multiplicity, and the Letters of Paul," 362.

reality and the propositional discourse of his letters. Johnson-DeBaufre rightly notes, however, that these stories are not actually in the letters themselves; they are not narrated by the writer but by scholars.[74]

The imposition of narrative is the imposition of meaning in response to a certain sense of anxiety. "The presence of [the] blank years in the annalist's account permits us to see, by way of contrast, the extent to which narrative strains for the effect of having filled in all the gaps, of having put an image of continuity, coherency, and meaning in place of the fantasies of emptiness, need, and frustrated desire that inhabit our nightmares about the destructive power of time."[75] But to supply such an image is to prefer the imaginary over the arguably more "real" and unembellished record of events. It is, in other words, to prefer a connotation of the real over its denotation. White's essay demonstrates that wherever narrativity is present in an account of reality, a moralizing impulse will accompany it; "that narrativizing discourse serves the purpose of moralizing judgements."[76] When the story elements of Phil. 3:4b-6 are fleshed out into a narrative plot that provides explanation and meaning, the narrative supplants the statements themselves. Even though the statements denote the real in a more concrete way as a chronological series of happenings, the narrative "makes the real desirable, makes the real into an object of desire . . . reality [now] wears the mask of a meaning."[77] Interpretation provides the second-order operation that moves us safely from the fragmentary, perpetually present discourse of what Barthes terms "the writerly" to the safety and comfort of its opposite: "the readerly," which is a product.[78] In the case of Philippians 3, what is produced is a clearly delimited past. For Barthes, this is a mode of commentary motivated by an ideology of totality.[79] For White, "the value of narrativity in the representation of real events arises out of a desire to have real events display the coherence, integrity, fullness, and closure of an image of life that is and can only be imaginary."[80]

---

[74] Ibid., 363.
[75] White, *Content of the Form*, 11.
[76] Ibid., 24.
[77] Ibid., 21.
[78] See Barthes, *S/Z*, 5.
[79] Ibid., 15.
[80] White, *Content of the Form*, 24.

So what then of the writer: How are we to understand the writer's work and the work of writing in this autobiographical vignette? In *Paul, the Corinthians, and the Birth of Christian Hermeneutics*, Margaret Mitchell writes:

> Given that Paul's heart is not an open book, or a visible or objective entity, Paul ensures his testimonial against [the Corinthians'] apparently misconstrued authorial intent by painting a retrospective self-portrait— of himself as letter writer, composing the controversial missive with tears streaming down his face. 2 Corinthians 2:4 contains in miniature a verbal self-portrait (the rhetorical form of *ekphrasis*) that is meant to torque the meaning of the prior words, to realign their meaning by juxtaposition with the disposition of the writer in the moment of composition.[81]

Much of what she says could apply just as well to what we encounter in Philippians 3. The writer is painting a very particular portrait of himself to serve as a kind of foil in juxtaposition to another version of himself which is constituted by the perspective it has of the former self. The autobiographical stories Paul narrates do not draw on the same materials scholars use in the narratives they tell, but rather take shape in the writer's own image-repertoire. "The self that is narrated is never an autonomously constituted self," writes Johnson-DeBaufre, "but one produced in relation, in the spaces between the self and others."[82] This resonates with what Barthes writes in his own autobiography, quoted above in Chapter 2. Speaking of both the book and himself as a character within it, he says: "He resists these ideas: his 'self' or ego, a rational concretion, ceaselessly resists them. Though consisting apparently of a series of 'ideas,' this book is not the book of his ideas; it is the book of the Self, the book of my resistances to my own ideas; it is a *recessive* book (which falls back, but which may also gain perspective thereby)."[83]

Barthes's autobiography is a useful intertext for reimagining the self-narration we encounter in Philippians 3. Linda Anderson describes it as an effort to "deconstruct from within the major assumptions underlying the genre."[84] As Barthes so often does in his work, he "rigorously eschews narrative

---

[81] Margaret Mitchell, *Paul, the Corinthians, and the Birth of Christian Hermeneutics* (Cambridge: Cambridge University Press, 2010), 102.

[82] Johnson-DeBaufre, "Narrative, Multiplicity, and the Letters of Paul," 367.

[83] Barthes, *Roland Barthes*, 119.

[84] Anderson, *Autobiography*, 66.

for the fragment,"[85] contending that "the important thing is that these little networks not be connected, that they not slide into a single enormous network which would be the structure of the book, its meaning."[86] Hence, "the book . . . offers repeated beginnings; not the reconstruction of a past nor a writing about the past but the continuing accretion, through the present act of writing, of new layers that work to 'abolish' his 'previous truth.'"[87] Anderson points out that the past is not merely jettisoned by Barthes so much as "it is stripped of its ideological function as a privileged source of meaning, as the 'natural' ground of identity."[88] Barthes "'freewheels' in language, collapsing the distinction between the present and the past; he creates a 'patchwork' of discursive fragments without reference to the past or the present; both equally constitute the 'surface' of the text in the 'here and now.'"[89]

Marcus notes that Barthes reflects the interests and tendencies of twentieth-century autobiographical writing in "following . . . the path of memories as they emerge to present consciousness, as opposed to their more conventional shaping into a linear time sequence."[90] Citing Michel Beaujour, she notes how *Roland Barthes by Roland Barthes* has a "thematic rather than a narrative structure, a kind of self-portrait 'in ink.'"[91] The visual plays a fundamental role in Barthes's autobiography. The book begins with a series of forty-three photographs, which he describes as "the figurations of the body's prehistory,"[92] after which follows what amounts to a collection, an assemblage, of fragments, vignettes, "which turn their back not only on chronology but on authorial identity."[93]

The writer of Phil. 3:4b-6 emerges in his relation to his image-repertoire. He describes himself as one no longer located in a meaningful past nor yet fully absorbed in an identifiable future. He is dis-located; he exists in dis-location. Because the self is fragmentary and a fiction, because any

[85] Ibid., 67.
[86] Barthes, *Roland Barthes*, 148.
[87] Anderson, *Autobiography*, 68, referencing Barthes, *Roland Barthes*, 56: "I do not say: 'I am going to describe myself' but: 'I am writing a text, and I call it R. B.'" and "I myself am my own symbol, I am the story which happens to me."
[88] Anderson, *Autobiography*, 68.
[89] Ibid.
[90] Marcus, *Autobiography*, 59.
[91] Ibid., 90.
[92] Barthes, *Roland Barthes*, 3. The first forty-two pages within which these photographs appear are not actually numbered. Noting the absence of pagination in the photographic collage, Anderson suggests that it is "just as psychologically the 'image-repertoire' could be said to precede, or be outside, writing" (*Autobiography*, 72).
[93] Marcus, *Autobiography*, 99. See also above 106, n. 71 regarding the "conclusion" of *Roland Barthes*.

narrative of the self requires being an Other to one's self for the purposes of narration, because the self is a refraction seen through the items that populate one's image-repertoire, what one ultimately owns or lays claim to in autobiographical writing is not an history or any concrete elements said to constitute an history, but only a particular relationship to the images of that history. Barthes says it this way: "What actually belongs to me is *my* image-repertoire, my phantasmatics."[94]

The writer of Philippians sees himself only in retrospect through the totality of the image-repertoire of both the past and the present. In listing the items of 3:4b-6, he refuses to cast forward the "weight of meaning . . . onto the future just beyond the immediate present."[95] Meanwhile, unwilling ourselves to refuse meaning, we imagine "Paul" as relatively coherent and complete. We supply a narrative that provides a meaning, a moral, and, most importantly, forces upon the writing (and the writer) an end, a conclusion, despite the writer's own unwillingness to speak of himself as anything other than fluid, incomplete, unfinished, perpetually straining toward. Returning to White, the impulse to supply a narrative to the list of Phil. 3:4b-6 betrays a fundamental distrust of and dissatisfaction with the form of history encountered in annals and, to a lesser extent, chronicles, which tend to be perceived as imperfect or incomplete.[96] But, according to White, such forms are themselves "particular products of possible conceptions of historical reality, conceptions that are alternatives to, rather than failed anticipations of, the fully realized historical discourse" that modern historiography presumes to embody.[97]

Arguably, then, Phil. 3:4b-6, and even the verses that follow, remind us that the fragment, the annals, the chronicle, is all there ever is, and in so doing they critique our own inclination to narrate the life of Paul. The writer's flattening of past and present strips both of their customary ideological function as privileged sources of meaning and as "natural" foundations of identity. Anderson notes that "for Barthes the most 'meaningful' discourse is discourse which does not allow itself to be 'caught,' but which 'rustles' with different meanings, with a *frisson* or excitation which moves language away

---

[94] Barthes, *Roland Barthes*, 152–53.
[95] White, *Content of the Form*, 22–23, referencing Frank Kermode, *The Sense of an Ending: Studies in the Theory of Fiction* (Oxford: Oxford University Press, 1967).
[96] White, *Content of the Form*, 4 and 5.
[97] Ibid., 5–6.

from definitive forms, from signs 'grimly weighted' by signifieds."[98] In Phil. 3:4b-6, I think we can detect just such a rustling, as well as a desire on the part of the writer to circumvent and resist any fixity imposed by connotation. If, as John Reumann suggests, the unique "I" of verses 3-7 shifts to an exemplary, paradigmatic "I" in verses 8 and following,[99] it is only at the expense of Paul himself. The real is exchanged for the imaginary as Paul is co-opted in service to a larger narrative.

However, as all narratives do, this one has within it the seeds of its own unraveling. Like Barthes, Paul has an abiding interest in the body.[100] In Phil. 3:8, he makes references to that which is bodily, to a sign or trace of the body's processes. He writes: "I have suffered the loss of all things, and I regard them as rubbish" (NRSV). Plenty of ink has been spilled on the word "rubbish," attempting to assign it a proper place in the narrative alongside everything else. But the word, especially in its less polite translations, has the power to produce an affect on the part of the reader and thereby to reconnect us to the real.[101]

A Lover's Discourse begins with a sort of preface in which Barthes describes the lover's discourse as something spoken but unwarranted, extremely isolated, out-of-sync with and cut off from so many other languages. "Once a discourse is thus driven by its own momentum into the backwater of the 'unreal,' exiled from all gregarity, it has no recourse but to become the site, however exiguous, of an *affirmation*."[102] That affirmation is the subject of *A Lover's Discourse*. The book is structured around a series of figures that refract in a fragmentary fashion instances of potential recognition on the part of the reader. "They utter the affect, then break off, their role is fulfilled."[103] These figures are dis-ordered, listed illogically: they are "non-syntagmatic, non-narrative," and therefore, like the lover himself, not integrated into a work.[104]

Barthes admits that "every amorous episode can be . . . endowed with a meaning: it is generated, develops, and dies; it is always possible to interpret

---

[98] Anderson, *Autobiography*, 69; referencing Barthes, *Roland Barthes*, 98.
[99] Reumann, *Philippians*, 518; citing J. Beker, *Paul: Apostle to the Gentiles* (Louisville: Westminster John Knox, 1993), 326. Reumann even acknowledges that any direct "application to the Philippians is not yet explicit, as in v 17 (voc. and impvs.). Only in retrospect, upon rereading, is Paul's story paradigmatic."
[100] Of particular note are Rom. 7:24; 1 Cor. 9:26-27; 2 Cor. 12:7; and Gal. 6:17.
[101] See Barthes, *Camera Lucida*; Anderson, *Autobiography*, 72.
[102] Barthes, *Lover's Discourse*, 1; emphasis in original.
[103] Ibid., 6.
[104] Ibid., 7.

according to a causality or a finality—even, if need be, which can be moralized."[105] He calls this the

> *love story*, subjugated to the great narrative Other, to that general opinion which disparages any excessive force and wants the subject himself to reduce the great imaginary current, the orderless, endless stream which is passing through him, to a painful, morbid crisis of which he must be cured . . . the love story . . . is the tribute the lover must pay to the world in order to be reconciled with it.[106]

What Barthes describes can easily apply, *mutatis mutandis*, to the narrated self, particularly as it is encountered in Philippians 1 and 3. In fact, it aptly describes the writer's discourse vis-à-vis the discourse on, of, and about "Paul." Whereas the letters reflect intermittent gestures of dialogue and contain within them instances—figures, if you will—of the writing-self, the myth of Paul is an effort at systemization and categorization that aims to reconcile the writer to the world. The writer's emotional exclamations, his being swept away in conversations not of his own choosing, his staging of the self according to certain images and narratives, his use of rhetorical devices to play his self in various guises, his appeal to familiar marks of identity, his gestures of longing and desire—especially vis-à-vis his confinement, his friends, and death—these are all matters of what Barthes called "tribute."

In the writings of Paul and in so many readings of those letters and of Paul we have a situation wherein "the other is absent as a referent, present as allocutory."[107] Speaking of the beloved as a fundamentally and perpetually absent Other, Barthes describes the oscillation between a desire for the absent being (*pothos*) and the even more intense desire for the being that is present (*himéros*).[108] But given that desire implies, indeed necessitates, an absence, the beloved is no less so in either case—the beloved is only ever not there. Even when physically present, the beloved is a source of anxiety premised on anticipated loss, a return to absence. Hence, "this singular distortion generates a kind of insupportable present: I am wedged between two tenses, that of the reference and that of the allocution."[109]

---

[105] Ibid.
[106] Ibid; emphasis in original.
[107] Ibid., 15.
[108] Cf. Fredrickson, *Eros and the Christ*, 11–34.
[109] Barthes, *Lover's Discourse*, 15.

Barthes later writes: "I have projected myself into the other with such power that when I am without the other I cannot recover myself, regain myself: I am lost, forever."[110] The comment plays in a variety of ways in the context of this study. Our writer is projected into so many characters throughout his self-narrations. He is also projected into those to whom he wrote, particularly in a letter like Philippians which bears the marks of affection and longing. And projections proliferate as subsequent readers desire to know the author, to ascertain and apprehend him. Barthes asks rhetorically: "To understand—is that not to divide the image, to undo the *I*, proud organ of misapprehension?"[111] In the self-narrations of Philippians, a writerly self-understanding emerges through unraveling and abandonment, through the undoing of the *I*. But we, too often in turn, seek to understand him as (i.e., in the form of) his projections into an Other. "Paul" is gone for good—his desire to depart fulfilled (1:23), all things lost (3:8). But the writer remains hard-pressed between presence and absence, dispersed and caught in an infinite network of relations, stretched across the surfaces of so many texts—the text of Philippians, the text of the corpus, the text of "Writer Paul."

---

[110] Ibid., 49.
[111] Ibid., 60.

Postscript: Writer Paul

The idea for this book emerged and took shape in much the same way as it unfolds in the pages above, which is to say somewhat randomly, arbitrarily, rhizomatically. Though born partly out of a growing fascination with Barthes and partly out of a growing frustration with the certainties, the assuredness that biblical scholars and ordinary readers alike profess about authors, works, meanings, and so forth—certainties that do not resonate with, much less match, my experience—it spread nonlinearly. The book has been a mildly experimental effort, an attempt to decenter Paul, but differently from the way others have done (e.g., Marchal, Johnson-DeBaufre, and Nasrallah)—namely, remaining as much as possible at the surface of the text.

In the novel *Possession*, the main character, Roland (interestingly enough), is said to regard letters as "a form of narrative that envisages no outcome, no closure. . . . Letters tell no story, because they do not know, from line to line, where they are going. . . . They exclude not only the reader as co-writer, or predictor, or guesser, but they exclude the reader as reader; they are written, if they are true letters, for *a* reader."[1] We are not the intended reader(s) of Paul's letters. We are voyeurs. There is no Author behind these letters; there is only a writer inscribed upon them, one who rustles among them, the grain of whose voice we hear as it passes away from him, away from us, away from any categories to which we would assign it in our effort to capture it. In order for that liveliness, that animation, to persist, we must resist the urge to make the letters works, no matter how pleasurable, and, instead, recognize and attend to instances of bliss. We must continually break up the crystallization of a name with all the connotations of thought, theology, and telos we associate and anchor with it. We must seek to circumvent whatever would assimilate the writer to *Doxa*, to myth. We must refuse the reduction of

---

[1] Byatt, *Possession*, 145; emphasis original.

the writerly to the readerly by always allowing for drift on the part of both the writer and ourselves when we aim to respond in kind.

At one point, a friend described what she sees me doing here as splashing in a stream, hopping from rock to rock, as opposed to diving deeply in one spot. I am fond of the image, even as I wrestle with the feeling that such writing lacks legitimacy. Nevertheless, it resonates with what characterizes so much of Barthes's writing. Sontag notes that Barthes was enamored with details, which she glosses as "experience's short form."[2] She describes his books as "multiples of short form rather than 'real' books, itineraries of topics rather than unified arguments."[3] Barthes was also deeply attracted to amateurism. Sontag describes him as "claiming and reclaiming amateur status . . . repeatedly disavow[ing] that, as it were, vulgar roles of system-builder, authority, mentor, expert, in order to reserve for himself the privileges and freedoms of delectation."[4] It is the perversity of a pleasure that possesses no self-evidently calculable benefit, the pleasure of what does not count according to whatever system would otherwise dictate value and significance.[5] Michael Moriarty sees it as a stance "against the ethic of violence and heroism," part of an "anti-heroic ethic of 'ease.'"[6] And Stafford notes that it was a fundamental component of Barthes's utopian vision "in which the 'amateur,' a creation 'in theory,' was 'disalienated.'"[7] Barthes's impulse is driven by democratic and ethical concerns. "For Barthes," writes Sontag, "it is not the commitment that writing makes to something outside of itself . . . that makes literature an instrument of opposition and subversion but a certain practice of writing itself: excessive, playful, intricate, subtle, sensuous—language which can never be that of power."[8] The combination of amateurism, drift, fragmentary writing, and so on results in an impressionistic effect insofar as it only ever provides a simulacrum of the subject and it draws attention to the writer. Jean Baudrillard is famously quoted as having said, "What I am, I don't know.

---

[2] Sontag, "Writing Itself," xiii. Among the fragments of Barthes's writing, he was drawn particularly to haiku and quotations.

[3] Ibid., xiii.

[4] Ibid., ix.

[5] See Stafford, *Phenomenon and Myth*, 202–4; Sontag, "Writing Itself," xiii.

[6] Moriarty, *Roland Barthes*, 182.

[7] Stafford, *Phenomenon and Myth*, 195. Stafford is referencing Barthes's essay, "The Grain of the Voice," wherein Barthes assigns the grain a "theoretical value" which is "the emergence of the text in the work," thereby establishing an alternative "scheme of evaluation" that is individual but not subjective (188).

[8] Ibid., xix.

I am the simulacrum of myself."[9] The simulacrum is all we ever have. Therefore, writing in such a way becomes its own form of responsible action.

The danger in "Barthes's radical inversion of the reader-author relationship," according to Bernard Poirot-Delpech, is that "students might marvel at the 'ease' with which Barthes the magician performed his 'trick', and be tempted simply to copy the maestro instead of establishing their own 'pleasures' of reading."[10] For as much as I enjoy reading Barthes and find his writing compelling, my goal has not been primarily to try replicating him or applying him to Paul and certain New Testament letters bearing his name in order to explain or interpret either them or their writer. My aim, in the readings I have performed, has been to follow the drift of my own intertexts, praising what I found praiseworthy irrespective of why, most of all in order to linger with the writing and writer as such, and then perhaps also to give voice to something too easily and frequently overlooked in readings that are more concerned with what is behind or what follows from either.

Nevertheless, there is another rationale for what I have done and the approach I have taken. I am persuaded that Barthes's preference for amateurism, drift, fragmentary writing befits any consideration of the writer of Romans, Corinthians, and Philippians because he also was an amateur, prone to drift, and fragmentary in the varieties of his topics and in the vagaries of the performances of his self. At the most fundamental level, we encounter this writer through a bricolage: an arbitrary and circumstantial collection of individual letters. Moreover, he never seems unaware of writing. Contrary to what Douglass Campbell argues,[11] we will never get to the bottom of the chronology, contingency, and coherence of these letters or their writer, thereby establishing firmly and reliably the linear development of the writer's life and thought. The biography we produce in molding and transforming the writer thus will only ever be "a novel which does not dare say its name."[12]

---

[9] Larissa MacFarquhar, "Baudrillard on Tour," *The New Yorker* (November 28, 2005) [https://www.ne wyorker.com/magazine/2005/11/28/baudrillard-on-tour].

[10] Cited in Stafford, *Phenomenon and Myth*, 179.

[11] Douglass A. Campbell, *Framing Paul: An Epistolary Biography* (Grand Rapids: Eerdmans, 2014). Cf. Michel Delville, "'At the Center, What?' *Giacomo Joyce*, Roland Barthes, and the Novelistic Fragment," *James Joyce Quarterly* 36 (1999): 765–80; Melanie Johnson-DeBaufre, "Historical Approaches: Which Past? Whose Past?" in *Studying Paul's Letters: Contemporary Perspectives and Methods*, ed. Joseph A. Marchal (Minneapolis: Fortress Press, 2012), 13–32.

[12] Roland Barthes, *OCii*, 1307; cited in and translated by Andy Stafford, *Roland Barthes: Phenomenon and Myth* (Edinburgh: Edinburgh University Press, 1988), 190f.

I have labeled this final chapter a postscript because there is no formal conclusion to make. The chapter contains no proper summary of the book's contents because there is no reduction. The Paul of Romans, Corinthians, and Philippians *is* his writing—or, rather, the Pauls of Romans, Corinthians, and Philippians are *their* writing. Each constitutes the other simultaneously. Neither precedes the other, and there is no accretion.

And yet, all is not lost, and something is perhaps even gained. Barthes saw the place and activity of writing as a space wherein the "I" can breathe, as it were. "Barthes can escape from the 'image-repertoire' in the space of work; words themselves, freed from their known place—their pigeon-holes—and attached to desire, can take the place of transitional objects."[13] Writer Paul seems similarly attuned to this in the passages I have read in this book. And it is Writer Paul that through letters we have effectively purloined, that sparks and kindles a relation of desire.

The end of *The Pleasure of the Text* begins with this: "If it were possible to imagine an aesthetic of textual pleasure, it would have to include: *writing aloud.*"[14] He explains that what he means by "writing aloud" is not expression (i.e., "dramatic inflections, subtle stresses, sympathetic accents," all of which remains beholden to the structure of rhetoric and to "the theatre of emotions"). Writing aloud is carried "by the *grain* of the voice, which is an erotic mixture of timbre and language, and can therefore also be, along with diction, the substance of an art: the art of guiding one's body."[15]

This aesthetic of textual pleasure, this erotics of text and textuality, this bliss, is material, raw, and sensual. It is ever-present but never captured. It is not subject to a grammar or syntax; it cannot be assimilated and thus translated. Writing aloud is in "the pulsional incidents, the language lined with flesh, a text where we can hear the grain of the throat, the patina of consonants, the voluptuousness of vowels, a whole carnal stereophany: the articulation of the body, of the tongue, not that of meaning, of language."[16] Such is the stuff of the writer one encounters in Romans, Corinthians, and Philippians—at least potentially. This is the writer's body inscribed upon the surface of the text—*if* one is inclined to look for it, to read these letters as texts of bliss, to listen for

13 Anderson, *Autobiography*, 69.
14 Barthes, *Pleasure*, 66.
15 Ibid.
16 Ibid., 66–67.

"the sound of speech *close up* (this is, in fact, the generalized definition of the 'grain' of writing) and . . . hear in their materiality, their sensuality, the breath, the gutturals, the fleshiness of the lips, a whole presence of the human muzzle . . . to succeed in shifting the signified a great distance and in throwing, so to speak, the anonymous body of the actor into my ear: it granulates, it crackles, it caresses, it grates, it cuts, it comes: that is bliss."[17]

Such will not accrue to produce a biography, a history, a narrative. They are the stuff of the novelistic, not myth.

---

[17] Ibid., 67.

Works Cited

Aichele, George. *The Control of Biblical Meaning: Canon as Semiotic Mechanism.* Harrisburg, PA: Trinity Press International, 2001.

Aichele, George. *Simulating Jesus: Reality Effects in the Gospels.* London: Equinox, 2011.

Alameddine, Rabih. *An Unnecessary Woman: A Novel.* New York: Grove Press, 2013.

Allen, Graham. *Roland Barthes.* London: Routledge, 2003.

Amossy, Ruth. "Introduction to the Study of Doxa." *Poetics Today*, 23 (2002): 369–94.

Anderson, Janice Capel. "Matthew, Mark, and Paul: The Vintage Sounds of the Implied Author," in *Bible and Theory: Essays in Honor of Stephen D. Moore.* Edited by K. Jason Coker and Scott S. Elliott. Lanham, MD: Lexington Books/Fortress Academic, 2020.

Anderson, Linda R. *Autobiography.* New Critical Idiom. London: Routledge, 2001.

Babcock, Williams, S., ed. *Paul and the Legacies of Paul.* Dallas: Southern Methodist University Press, 1990.

Badmington, Neil. *The Afterlives of Roland Barthes.* London: Bloomsbury Academic, 2016.

Bal, Mieke. *Narratology: Introduction to the Theory of Narrative*, 2nd edn. Toronto: University of Toronto Press, 1997.

Barthes, Roland. "Barthes to the Third Power." 1975. In *On Signs*, 189–91. Edited by Marshall Blonsky. Baltimore: Johns Hopkins University Press, 1985.

Barthes, Roland. *Camera Lucida: Reflections on Photography.* Translated by Richard Howard. New York: Hill & Wang, 1981.

Barthes, Roland. *The Eiffel Tower and Other Mythologies.* Translated by Richard Howard. New York: Hill & Wang, 1979.

Barthes, Roland. *How to Live Together: Novelistic Simulations of Some Everyday Spaces.* Translated by Kate Briggs. European Perspectives. New York: Columbia University Press, 2002.

Barthes, Roland. *Image/Music/Text.* Translated by Stephen Heath. New York: Hill & Wang, 1977.

Barthes, Roland. *A Lover's Discourse: Fragments.* Translated by Richard Howard. New York: Hill & Wang, 1978.

Barthes, Roland. *Michelet.* 1954. Translated by Richard Howard. Berkeley: University of California Press, 1992.

Barthes, Roland. *Mourning Diary: October 26, 1977—September 15, 1979*. Translated by Richard Howard. New York: Hill & Wang, 2010.

Barthes, Roland. *Mythologies: The Complete Edition, in a New Translation*, translated by Richard Howard and Annette Lavers. 1957. New York: Hill & Wang, 2012.

Barthes, Roland. *The Neutral: Lecture Course at the Collège de France (1977–1978)*. Translated by Rosalind E. Krauss and Denis Hollier. European Perspectives. New York: Columbia University Press, 2005.

Barthes, Roland. *On Racine*. 1963. Translated by Richard Miller. New York: Hill & Wang, 1964.

Barthes, Roland. *The Pleasure of the Text*. Translated by Richard Howard. New York: Hill & Wang, 1975.

Barthes, Roland. *The Preparation of the Novel: Lecture Courses and Seminars at the Collège de France (1978–1979 and 1979–1980)*. Translated by Kate Briggs. European Perspectives. New York: Columbia University Press, 2010.

Barthes, Roland. *Roland Barthes by Roland Barthes*. Translated by Richard Howard. Berkeley: University of California Press, 1977.

Barthes, Roland. *The Rustle of Language*. Translated by Richard Howard. Berkeley: University of California Press, 1989.

Barthes, Roland. *S/Z: An Essay*. 1970. Translated by Richard Miller. New York: Hill & Wang, 1974.

Barthes, Roland. *Writing Degree Zero*. 1953. Translated by Annette Lavers and Colin Smith. New York: Hill & Wang, 1967.

Beker, J. *Paul: Apostle to the Gentiles*. Louisville: Westminster John Knox, 1993.

Berlant, Lauren. *Cruel Optimism*. Durham: Duke University Press, 2011.

Betz, Hans Dieter. *Der Apostel Paulus und die sokratische Tradition. Eine exegetische Untersuchung zu einer "Apologie" 2 Korinther 10–13*. Beiträge zur historischen Theologie 45. Tübingen: Mohr, 1972.

Betz, Hans Dieter. *Galatians: A Commentary on Paul's Letter to the Churches in Galatia*. Hermeneia. Philadelphia: Fortress Press, 1979.

Bird, Michael. *An Anomalous Jew: Paul among Jews, Greeks, and Romans*. Grand Rapids: Eerdmans, 2016.

Black, David Alan. *Paul, Apostle of Weakness: Astheneia and Its Cognates in the Pauline Literature*. Rev. edn. Eugene, OR: Pickwick Publications, 2012.

Bockmuehl, Markus. *The Epistle to the Philippians*. Black's New Testament Commentary. Peabody, MA: Hendrickson Publishers, 1998.

Bornkamm, Günther. "The Missionary Stance of Paul in 1 Corinthians 9 and in Acts." In *Studies in Luke-Acts: Essays Presented in Honor of Paul Schubert*, 194–207. Edited by L. E. Keck and J. L. Martyn. Nashville: Abingdon Press, 1966.

Bornkamm, Günther. *Paul*. Translated by D.M.G. Stalker. New York: Harper & Row, 1971.

Boyarin, Daniel. *A Radical Jew: Paul and the Politics of Identity.* Contraversions: Critical Studies in Jewish Literature, Culture, and Society. Berkeley: University of California Press, 1994.

Busch, Austin. "The Figure of Eve in Romans 7:5–25." *BibInt* 12 (2004): 1–36.

Byatt, A. S. *Possession: A Romance.* New York: Random House, 1990.

Campbell, Douglass A. *Framing Paul: An Epistolary Biography.* Grand Rapids: Eerdmans, 2014.

Castelli, Elizabeth A. *Imitating Paul: A Discourse of Power.* Louisville: Westminster John Knox, 1991.

Chadwick, Henry, "'All Things to All Men' (I Cor. ix.22)." *NTS* 1 (1954–1955): 261–75.

Conzelmann, Hans. *1 Corinthians.* Hermeneia. Philadelphia: Fortress Press, 1975.

Craddock, Fred. *Philippians.* Interpretation. Atlanta: John Knox, 1985.

Cranfield, C. E. B. *Romans.* International Critical Commentary Series. 2 vols. Edinburgh: T&T Clark, 1975.

Crossley, James G. *Reading the New Testament: Contemporary Approaches.* Reading Religious Texts. London: Routledge, 2010.

Croy, N. Clayton. "'To Die Is Gain' (Philippians 1:19-26): Does Paul Contemplate Suicide?" *JBL* 122 (2003): 517–31.

Culler, Jonathan. *Barthes: A Very Short Introduction.* Oxford: Oxford University Press, 1983.

Delville, Michel. "'At the Center, What?' *Giacomo Joyce*, Roland Barthes, and the Novelistic Fragment." *James Joyce Quarterly* 36 (1999): 765–80.

de Man, Paul. "Autobiography as De-Facement." *Modern Language Notes* 94 (1979): 919–30.

Derrida, Jacques. "The Deaths of Roland Barthes." In *The Work of Mourning*, 31–68. Edited by Pascale-Anne Brault and Michael Naas. Chicago: University of Chicago Press, 2001.

Derrida, Jacques. *Mémoires pour Paul de Man.* Paris: Galilée, 1988.

Dougherty, Darrell J. "Citizens of Heaven. Philippians 3:2-21 as a Deutero-Pauline Passage." *NTS* 41 (1995): 102–22.

Droge, J. A., and J. D. Tabor. *A Noble Death.* San Francisco: HarperCollins, 1992.

Dunn, Mark. *Ibid: A Life.* San Francisco: MacAdam/Cage, 2004.

Elder, Nicholas. Review of Will N. Timmins, *Romans 7 and Christian Identity: A Study of the 'I' in Its Literary Context*, *Review of Biblical Literature* [http://www. bookreviews.org] (2019).

Elder, Nicholas. "'Wretch I Am!' Eve's Tragic Speech-in-Character in Romans 7:7-25." *JBL* 137 (2018): 743–63.

Elliott, Scott S. "What Is Paul? Mythology and the Neutral in 1 Corinthians 9.19-23." In *Simulating Aichele: Essays in Bible, Film, Culture and Theory*, 120–39. Edited by Melissa C. Stewart. Sheffield: Sheffield Phoenix Press, 2015.

Ellis, E. Earle. "Coworkers, Paul and His." In *Dictionary of Paul and His Letters*, 183–89. Edited by Gerald F. Hawthorne, Ralph P. Martin, and Daniel G. Reid. Downers Grove, IL: InterVarsity Press, 1993.

Fee, Gordon D. *The First Epistle to the Corinthians*. New International Commentary on the New Testament. Grand Rapids: Eerdmans, 1987.

Fee, Gordon D. *Paul's Letter to the Philippians*. New International Commentary on the New Testament. Grand Rapids: Eerdmans, 1995.

Felman, Shoshana. *What Does a Woman Want?: Reading and Sexual Difference*. Baltimore: Johns Hopkins University Press, 1993.

Ferguson, Sam. *Diaries Real and Fictional in Twentieth-Century French Writing*. Oxford: Oxford University Press, 2018.

Fewster, Gregory P. "'Can I Have Your Autograph?': On Thinking about Pauline Authorship and Pseudepigraphy." *Bulletin for the Study of Religion* 43/3 (2014): 30–39.

Flemming, Dean. *Philippians: A Commentary in the Wesleyan Tradition*. Kansas City: Beacon Hill Press, 2009.

Foucault, Michel. "Technologies of the Self." In *Technologies of the Self: A Seminar with Michel Foucault*, 16–49. Edited by Luther H. Martin, Huck Gutman, and Patrick H. Hutton. Amherst: University of Massachusetts Press, 1988.

Foucault, Michel. "What Is an Author?" 1979. In *The Foucault Reader*, 101–20. Edited by Paul Rabinow. New York: Pantheon Books, 1984.

Fowl, Stephen. *Philippians*. Two Horizons New Testament Commentary. Grand Rapids: Eerdmans, 2005.

Fowl, Stephen. "The Use of Scripture in Philippians." In *Paul and Scripture: Extending the Conversation*, 163–84 Edited by Christopher D. Stanley (Atlanta: Society of Biblical Literature, 2012).

Fredrickson, David E. *Eros and the Christ: Longing and Envy in Paul's Christology*. Minneapolis: Fortress Press, 2013.

Furnish, Victor Paul. *II Corinthians: A New Translation with Introduction and Commentary*. The Anchor Bible 32A. Garden City: Doubleday & Company, 1984.

Gallop, Jane. *The Deaths of the Author: Reading and Writing in Time*. Durham: Duke University Press, 2011.

Gaventa, Beverly R. "Galatians 1 and 2: Autobiography as Paradigm." *NovT* 28 (1986): 309–26.

Genette, Gérard. *Narrative Discourse: An Essay in Method*. Translated by Jane E. Lewin. Ithaca, NY: Cornell University Press, 1980.

Genette, Gérard. *Narrative Discourse Revisited*. Translated by Jane E. Lewin. Ithaca, NY: Cornell University Press, 1988.

Gide, André. *Journals Volume 1: 1889–1913*. Translated by Justin O'Brien. Urbana: University of Illinois Press, 1947.

Gil, Marie. "Roland Barthes: Life as a Text." Translated by Sam Ferguson. *Barthes Studies* 1 (2015): 35–60.

Gooder, Paula R. *Only the Third Heaven? 2 Corinthians 12.1–10 and Heavenly Ascent.* Library of New Testament Studies 313. Edited by Mark Goodacre. London: T&T Clark, 2006.

Goulder, Michael. "Vision and Knowledge." *JSNT* 56 (1994): 53–71.

Grosheide, F. W. *Commentary on the First Epistle to the Corinthians.* New International Commentary on the New Testament. Grand Rapids: Eerdmans, 1953.

Halberstam, Judith. *The Queer Art of Failure*. Durham: Duke University Press, 2011.

Hamilton, John. *Philology of the Flesh*. Chicago: The University of Chicago Press, 2018.

Haraway, Donna. "Situated Knowledges: The Science Question in Feminism and the Privilege of Partial Perspective." In *Feminist Theory Reader*, 441–51. Edited by Carole R. McCann and Seung-Kyung Kim. 4th edn. New York: Routledge, 2017.

Hawthorne, Jeremy. *A Concise Dictionary of Contemporary Literary Theory*. London: Arnold, 1992.

Héring, Jean. *The First Epistle of Saint Paul to the Corinthians*. Translated by A. W. Heathcote and P. J. Alcock; London: The Epworth Press, 1962.

Herman, David. *Story Logic: Problems and Possibilities of Narrative*. Lincoln: University of Nebraska Press, 2002.

Holloway, Paul A. *Philippians*. Hermeneia. Minneapolis: Fortress Press, 2017.

Horsley, Richard A., ed. *Paul and Empire: Religion and Power in Roman Imperial*. Harrisburg, PA: Trinity Press International, 1997.

Jahn, Manfred. "Focalization." In *The Cambridge Companion to Narrative*, 94–108. Edited by David Herman. Cambridge: Cambridge University Press, 2007.

Jewett, Robert. *Romans*. Hermeneia. Minneapolis: Fortress Press, 2007.

Johnson-DeBaufre, Melanie. "Historical Approaches: Which Past? Whose Past?" In *Studying Paul's Letters: Contemporary Perspectives and Methods*, 13–32. Edited by Joseph A. Marchal. Minneapolis: Fortress Press, 2012.

Johnson-DeBaufre, Melanie. "Narrative, Multiplicity, and the Letters of Paul." In *The Oxford Handbook of Biblical Narrative*, 362–375. Edited by Danna Nolan Fewell. Oxford: Oxford University Press, 2016.

Johnson-DeBaufre, Melanie, and Laura S. Nasrallah. "Beyond the Heroic Paul: Toward a Feminist and Decolonizing Approach to the Letters of Paul." In *The Colonized Apostle: Paul through Postcolonial Eyes*, 161–74. Edited by Christopher D. Stanley. Minneapolis: Fortress Press, 2011.

Keener, Craig S. *1–2 Corinthians*. The New Cambridge Bible Commentary. Cambridge: Cambridge University Press, 2005.

Kermode, Frank. *The Sense of an Ending: Studies in the Theory of Fiction*. Oxford: Oxford University Press, 1967.

Keskinen, Mikko. "Blocks to, and Building Blocks of, Narrativity: Fragments, Anecdotes, and Narrative Lines in David Markson's Reader's Block." *Frontiers of Narrative Studies* 3 (2017): 224–37.

Kim, Seyoon. *Paul and the New Perspective: Second Thoughts on the Origin of Paul's Gospel*. Grand Rapids: Eerdmans, 2001.

Knight, Diana. *Barthes and Utopia: Space, Travel, Writing*. Oxford: Clarendon Press, 1997.

Koester, Helmut. "The Purpose of the Polemic of a Pauline Fragment (Philippians iii)." *NTS* 8 (1961–1962): 317–32.

Lambrecht, Jan. *The Wretched "I" and Its Liberation: Paul in Romans 7 and 8*. Grand Rapids: Eerdmans, 1992.

Lincoln, Andrew T. "'Paul the Visionary': The Setting and Significance of the Rapture to Paradise in II Corinthians XII.1-10." *NTS* 25 (1979): 204–20.

Lyons, George. *Pauline Autobiography: Toward a New Understanding*. SBL Dissertation Series 73. Atlanta: Society of Biblical Literature, 1985.

MacFarquhar, Larissa. "Baudrillard on Tour." *The New Yorker* (November 28, 2005) [https://www.newyorker.com/magazine/2005/11/28/baudrillard-on-tour].

Madruga, John. "Roland Barthes on the Tour," *Peloton* 5 (August–September, 2011): 100–105.

Marchal, Joseph A. *The Politics of Heaven: Women, Gender, and Empire in the Study of Paul*. Minneapolis: Fortress Press, 2008.

Marcus, Laura. *Autobiography: A Very Short Introduction*. Oxford: Oxford University Press, 2018.

Markson, David. *Reader's Block*. Champaign, IL: Dalkey Archive Press, 1996.

Markson, David. *Wittgenstein's Mistress*. Champaign, IL: Dalkey Archive Press, 1988.

Matlock, R. Barry. "Almost Cultural Studies? Reflections on the 'New Perspective' on Paul." In *Biblical Studies/Cultural Studies: The Third Sheffield Colloquium*, 433–59. Edited by J. Cheryl Exum and Stephen D. Moore. JSOT Supp. Ser. 266. Gender, Culture, Theory 7. Sheffield: Sheffield Academic Press, 1998.

Mitchell, David. *Cloud Atlas: A Novel*. New York: Random House, 2004.

Mitchell, Margaret M. *Paul, the Corinthians and the Birth of Christian Hermeneutics*. Cambridge: Cambridge University Press, 2010.

Moore, Stephen D. *Gospel Jesuses and Other Nonhumans: Biblical Criticism Post-Poststructuralism*. Semeia Studies 89. Atlanta: Society of Biblical Literature, 2017.

Moriarty, Michael. *Roland Barthes*. Stanford: Stanford University Press, 1991.

Morray-Jones, C. R. A. "Paradise Revisited (2 Cor 12:1-12): The Jewish Mystical Background of Paul's Apostolate. Part 1: The Jewish Sources." *HTR* 86 (1993): 177–217.

Morray-Jones, C. R. A. "Paradise Revisited (2 Cor 12:1-12): The Jewish Mystical Background of Paul's Apostolate. Part 2: Paul's Heavenly Ascent and Its Significance." *HTR* 86 (1993): 265–92.

Nikki, Nina. "The Flexible Apostle: Paul's Varied Social Identification in 1 Corinthians 9 and Philippians 3." In *Others and the Construction of Early Christian Identities*, 75–101. Edited by Raimo Hakola, Nina Nikki, and Ulla Tervahauta. Publications of the Finnish Exegetical Society 106. Helsinki: The Finnish Exegetical Society, 2013.

Nikki, Nina. *Opponents and Identity in Philippians*. Supplements to Novum Testamentum 173. Leiden: Brill, 2019.

O'Brien, Peter T. *The Epistle to the Philippians: A Commentary on the Greek Text. New International Greek Testament Commentary*. Grand Rapids: Eerdmans, 1991.

O'Brien, Sharon. "Feminist Theory and Literary Biography." In *Contesting the Subject. Essays in the Postmodern Theory and Practice of Biography and Biographical Criticism*, 123–33. Edited by William H. Epstein. West Lafayette, IN: Purdue University Press, 1991.

O'Neill, Patrick. *Fictions of Discourse: Reading Narrative Theory*. Toronto: University of Toronto Press, 1996.

Orr, William F., and James Arthur Walther. *1 Corinthians*. Anchor Bible, vol. XXXII. Garden City, NY: Doubleday, 1976.

Pontalis, J.-B. *Love of Beginnings*. 1986. Translated by James Greene with Marie-Christine Réguis. London: Free Association Books, 1993.

Price, Brian. *A Theory of Regret*. Durham: Duke University Press, 2017.

Reumann, John. *Philippians: A New Translation with Introduction and Commentary*. Anchor Yale Bible 33B. New Haven: Yale University Press, 2008.

Richardson, P. "Pauline Inconsistency: I Corinthians 9:19-23 and Galatians 2:11-14." *NTS* 26 (1979/80): 347–62.

Rimmon-Kenan, Shlomith. *Narrative Fiction: Contemporary Poetics*. 2nd edn. London: Methuen, 2002.

Sampley, J. Paul. "The First Letter to the Corinthians: Introduction, Commentary, and Reflections." In *The New Interpreter's Bible* vol. X, 771–1003. Edited by Leander E. Keck. Nashville: Abingdon Press, 2002.

Sampley, J. Paul. "The Second Letter to the Corinthians: Introduction, Commentary, and Reflections." In *The New Interpreter's Bible*, vol. XI, 1–180. Edited by Leander E. Keck. Nashville: Abingdon Press, 2000.

Sampley, J. Paul. *Walking between the Times: Paul's Moral Reasoning*. Minneapolis: Fortress Press, 1986.

Sampley, J. Paul. "The Weak and the Strong: Paul's Careful and Crafty Rhetorical Strategy in Romans 14:1–15:13." In *The Social World of the First Christians: Essays in Honor of Wayne A. Meeks*, 40–52. Edited by L. Michael White and O. Larry Yarbrough; Minneapolis: Fortress Press, 1995.

Sartre, Jean-Paul. *Nausea*. 1938. Translated by Lloyd Alexander. Harmondsworth, Middlesex: Penguin, 1965.

Schütz, John Howard. *Paul and the Anatomy of Apostolic Authority*. 1975. Louisville: Westminster John Knox, 2007.

Seifrid, Mark A. "The Subject of Rom 7:14-25," *NovT* 34 (1992): 313–33.

Smith, Jonathan Z. "Sacred Persistence: Toward a Redescription of Canon." In *Imagining Religion: From Babylon to Jonestown*, 36–52. Chicago: University of Chicago Press, 1982.

Sontag, Susan, ed. *A Roland Barthes Reader*. 1982. New York: Barnes & Noble, 2009.

Stafford, Andy. *Roland Barthes, Phenomenon and Myth: An Intellectual Biography*. Edinburgh: Edinburgh University Press, 1998.

Stafford, Andy. *Roland Barthes*. Critical Lives. London: Reaktion Books, 2015.

Stendahl, Krister. "The Apostle Paul and the Introspective Conscience of the West." *HTR* 56 (1963): 199–215.

Stowers, Stanley K. *A Rereading of Romans: Justice, Jews, and Gentiles*. New Haven: Yale University Press, 1994.

Tabor, James D. *Things Unutterable: Paul's Ascent to Paradise in Its Greco-Roman, Judaic, and Early Christian Contexts*. Studies in Judaism. Lanham, MD: University Press of America, 1986.

Tamez, Elsa., Cynthia Briggs, Kittredge., Claire, Colombo. and Alicia J. Batten, "Philippians." In, *Philippians, Colossians, Philemon*, 1–122. Wisdom Commentary 51. Collegeville, MN: Liturgical Press, 2017.

Teeuwen, Rudolphus, "An Epoch of Rest: Roland Barthes's 'Neutral' and the Utopia of Weariness." *Cultural Critique* 80 (2012): 1–26.

Timmins, Will N. *Romans 7 and Christian Identity: A Study of the 'I' in Its Literary Context*. Society for the Study of the New Testament Monograph Series 170. Cambridge: Cambridge University Press, 2017.

Tofighi, Fatima. *Paul's Letters and the Construction of the European Self*. Scriptural Traces: Critical Perspectives on the Reception and Influence of the Bible 10. London: Bloomsbury, 2017.

Touponce, William. "Literary Theory and the Notion of Difficulty." In *The Idea of Difficulty in Literature*, 51–72. Edited by Alan C. Purves. Albany: SUNY Press, 1991.

Troftgruben, Troy. "The Gravitas of Letters: Intra-Diegetic Epistles in Jewish, Greek, and Christian Narratives." Annual Meeting of the Society of Biblical Literature, Ancient Fiction and Early Christian and Jewish Narrative Section. Atlanta, GA, November 2015.

Twomey, Jay. "'Though We May Seem to Have Failed': Paul and Failure in Steve Ross' *Blinded*." In *Reading with Feeling: Affect Theory and the Bible*. Edited by Fiona Black and Jennifer Koosed. Atlanta: Semeia Studies (Forthcoming).

Waggoner, Matt. *Unhoused: Adorno and the Problem of Dwelling*. New York: Columbia University Press, 2018.

Wallace, David Foster. *Both Flesh and Not: Essays*. New York: Back Bay Books, 2012.

White, Hayden. *The Content of the Form: Narrative Discourse and Historical Representation*. Baltimore: The Johns Hopkins University Press, 1987.

White, Hayden. "The Value of Narrativity in the Representation of Reality." *Critical Inquiry*, 7/1 (1980): 5–27.

Witherington, Ben. *Paul's Letter to the Philippians: A Socio-Rhetorical Commentary*. Grand Rapids: Eerdmans, 2011.

Witherington, Ben. *Paul's Letter to the Romans: A Socio-Rhetorical Commentary*. Grand Rapids: Eerdmans, 2011.

Wouk, Herman. *The Lawgiver*. New York: Simon and Schuster, 2012.

Index

CPSIA information can be obtained
at www.ICGtesting.com
Printed in the USA
LVHW080158281221
707334LV00007B/191

9 780567 703156